Becoming a BLACK WOMAN

2nd Edition

By Dr. Ruth D. Edwards

BECOMING A BLACK WOMAN, 2nd Edition
Published By Dr. Ruth D. Edwards

Book Cover and Interior Design by Big Easy Creative

ISBN: 979-8-9916202-1-5

Produced and Printed in the United States of America

10 9 8 7 6 5 4 3 2

Becoming a BLACK WOMAN

2nd Edition

By Dr. Ruth D. Edwards

In Memoriam

Edna Dorothy Porcher Edwards

Daisy Joanne Edwards Harris

Brenda Solese Porcher Gilchrist Howard

Dedication

I dedicate this work to the Black women in my life, the ones who came before, those I walk with, and those who come behind. I hope that this work sheds some light in the personal places where questions may linger about "how we got to be this way." This is also dedicated to the Black men in my life, past and present, who were and are my heroes and protectors. I hope this work honors the memories of those who are gone and enlightens interactions with Black women for those still here.

To the memory of my maternal and paternal grandparents. They did the best they could with the knowledge they had to make a world for their children and the generations that followed. Each one valued education and knowledge as the keys to success. Thank you for dreaming a world for all of us. We are your wildest dreams; I hope we are making you proud.

To the community of Black women academics at Fielding Graduate University, thank you for modeling what Black women across generations have always done well: love, sustain, and support each other. To Dr. Charlyn Green Fareed and Some Time With My Sistahs Black Women's Retreat for the healing weekends you provided and that we all needed.

Lastly, to Alyce, Barbara, Bernadette, Bernice, Diane, Ebony, and Joyce, thanks to each of you for joining me on this journey. The work we engaged in established a window for how to view Black women within the context of US society. Thank you for sharing pieces of yourself with me and allowing me to share myself with you. Finally, to John, I especially thank you for your insight, your coaching, and the retreat at Wolf Laurel. Namasté.

Table of Contents

Chapter 1: Introduction

> *"The field of psychology does not holistically address black women. Black psychology has a male centered focus. The complexity of racism and sexism is rarely incorporated into research, disallowing black women from gaining full representation in this field. Feminist and Black psychology do not fully include black women in their foundation – hence research on them remains scant."*
>
> *(Gurira, 2001, p. 5)*

I am a Black heterosexual woman, raised Christian in Awendaw, South Carolina. I am also the middle of five children born to a registered nurse and a self-educated small-business owner. We lived in Awendaw, South Carolina, populated predominantly by Black and White families. My siblings and I attended private Catholic school 25 miles away in the City of Charleston. As early as I can remember, I have been conscious of my skin color and my gender.

I was also raised middle class, based on my observation of what we had that others didn't. My maternal grandfather gifted the two acres of land that held my childhood home – a two-story house with my father's business attached to the front. We had a huge back yard and a double garage with two cars in it. How did this background influence my development as a Black girl growing up in US society? The primary question of this study is to determine how lived experience influences development for Black women born and raised in the United States. I am most curious to determine how Black girls navigate the intersections of race, gender and class to become Black women.

I grew up in rural South Carolina. My father owned a full service gas station on highway seventeen, north. Instead of paved sidewalks, there was the open highway with a walking path alongside; in place of street lamps, the highway was dotted with equally spaced light poles. Our closest neighbors were my maternal grandmother who lived a quarter mile 'up the road' and our local post office located about the same distance 'down the road'.

At the age of ten, it became my job to walk to the post office on Saturday mornings to pick up the mail. As I made the return trip on this particular sunny Saturday morning, I noticed a blue pick-up truck coming down the highway. As it approached, I could see three young White men inside. The truck slowed as it neared me and one of them hurled a small lunch bag of trash at me out of the passenger window while all three of them yelled something unintelligible. I froze, afraid to turn around; I listened for the sound of the truck stopping. It kept going.

Home was a short distance away as I could see the gas tanks at my father's station, but Daddy wasn't in sight. I calmed myself and got home as quickly as I could. I don't recall anything specific about returning home – only that I was just relieved to be safe back in my parents' house. I never told my parents about this incident. What does a Black girl child do with this experience? For reasons I've yet to understand, I kept silent.

It was rural South Carolina in the early '60's and I recognized racism when I saw it. I'd heard the story of my great-grandfather being shot trying to protect his son. I knew the story of my grandfather putting his brother on a northbound Greyhound bus at midnight to avoid his being lynched. The March on Washington had passed through Charleston and stopped at my elementary school where kitchen staff served the marchers breakfast. When I remember it, I can still smell the aroma of scrambled eggs.

When I decided to pursue my doctoral degree, I knew instinctively that I would study some aspect of Black womanhood. Growing up, I was surrounded by courageous, intelligent, righteous women – my mother, grandmothers, sisters, and aunts. Each had her own style and manner of moving through the world. I also grew up seeing Black women often diminished in their day-to-day interactions by other Black people, and by members of the dominant culture. This research path is a logical one for me.

My whole life, I have wondered what makes us [Black women] behave the way we do. I'm the second of four daughters. Despite being raised in the same home, our birth-to-adult life experiences are very different, from each other's perspective. According to Lewin, *behavior* is a *function* of the *person* in the *environment: B =F (P, E).* My behavior is partly determined by my role in US society. It is colored by my being Black, female, heterosexual, Southern-born, middle-class, mostly able-bodied, and Christian. My socially defined roles are part of this formula as well: daughter, niece, sister, aunt, cousin, friend, student and employee.

Parham, White and Ajamu (2000) maintain that Black people learn to view themselves based on what they are told about their place in the world, who the world says they are, and how they behave in the context of that world. Collins (2000) states: "the convergence of race, gender and class oppression characteristic of US slavery shaped all subsequent relationships that women of African descent had within Black families and communities, with employers and among one another" (p. 4). From the moment of birth, Black women's lived experience unfolds amid these three layers. My inquiry focuses on what happens from the point she first realizes she is Black, female and different.

What defines us as a social group? Who had "power to name" with respect to these definitions? What does my behavior look like in the context of ascribed social group roles? How does my behavior mirror that of other US born Black women in similar roles? These questions are one part of the impetus for this study.

Statement of the Problem

> *"That man over there says that women need to be helped into carriages, and lifted over ditches, and to have the best place everywhere. Nobody ever helps me into carriages, or over mud-puddles, or gives me any best place! Ain't I a woman?"*
>
> *(Truth, 1851, p. 1)*

The history of Black women in the United States is a litany of oppression through physical and verbal abuse and marginalization and the distress of it continues today. "A devaluation of black womanhood occurred as a result of the sexual exploitation of black women during slavery that has not altered in the course of hundreds of years" (hooks, 1981). This study is about exploring our past as a means of self-healing through reflection and self-reflection. It is also about using the lessons learned from this experience to define ourselves, for ourselves.

Significance of the Study

> *"One discovers what it means to be Black and all that the term implies, usually outside the family."*
>
> *(Lindsey, 1970, p. 87)*

Lindsey's quote supports the perception of some Black women's early childhood experience. From birth to school age, my familiars all looked like me. I became accustomed to their behaviors, their voices and everything about them. They were my reality; it was only when I stepped outside of my cultural comfort zone that I was questioned, derided and assumed not to be normal. This assumption of abnormality is historical for both the oppressor and the oppressed.

A document entitled the *Full Text of the Willie Lynch Writings*[1] represents instructions for breaking the spirit of Black people. There are questions about the existence of Mr. Lynch and the validity of the document. However, it has come curiously close to describing some of what I perceive as present-day challenges facing Black women in the United States today. Here is what this document proposes for "handling" the Black woman in US society:

> *"THE BREAKING PROCESS OF THE AFRICAN WOMAN*
>
> *Take the female and run a series of tests on her to see if she will submit to your desires willingly. Test her in every way, because she is the most important factor for good economics. If she shows any signs of resistance in submitting completely to your will, do not hesitate to use the bullwhip on her – to extract that last bit of bitch out of her. Take care not to kill her, for in doing so you spoil good economics. When in complete submission, she will train her offspring in the early years to submit to labor when they become of age. Understanding is the best thing. Therefore, we shall go deeper into this area of the subject matter concerning what we have produced here in this breaking of the female nigger. We have reversed the relationship. In her natural uncivilized state, she would have a strong dependency on the uncivilized nigger male, and she would have a limited protective dependency toward her independent male offspring and would raise female offspring to be dependent like her. Nature had provided*

1 While the source of this document cannot be validated, it's commonly referred to for its social prescription regarding the acculturation of African heritage people in the United States.

for this type of balance. We reversed nature by burning and pulling one civilized nigger apart and bullwhipping the other to the point of death – all in her presence. By her being left alone, unprotected, with male image destroyed, the ordeal caused her to move from her psychological dependent state to a frozen independent state. In this frozen psychological state of independence, she will raise her male and female offspring in reversed roles. For fear of the young male's life, she will psychologically train him to be mentally weak and dependent, but physically strong. Because she has become psychologically independent, she will train her female offspring to be psychologically independent as well. What have you got? You've got the nigger woman out front, and the nigger man behind and scared"

(Lynch, 1712).

Notions that are raised in this document of a "frozen independent state" resonate with me as part of our lived experience. For generations, Black women have steeled themselves to survive numerous atrocities: rape, mental and physical abuse and the loss of children and/or husband to death or the auction block. I wonder what it was like to wake up each morning wondering if you, your husband or child would be sold that day. Linda Brent (Brent, 1973) recounts such a situation in her memoir, *Incidents in the Life of a Slave Girl:*

On one of these sale days, I saw a mother lead seven children to the auction-block. She knew that some of them would be taken from her; but they took all. The children were sold to a slave trader and the mother was bought by a man in her own town. I met that mother in the street, and her wild haggard face lives to-day in my mind. She wrung her hands in anguish, and exclaimed, "Gone! All gone! Why don't God kill me?" I had no words wherewith to comfort her. Instances of this kind are of daily, yea, of hourly occurrence" (1973, p. 14).

I propose that the trauma of managing this type of distress and related ordeals forced the enslaved Black woman to embrace this "frozen independent state." In essence, she shut down some piece of herself; turned it off, so to speak, so she could keep living, no matter what. She was forced to create methods for salvaging her sanity for herself, realizing that even if she cried out for help, "none but Jesus heard me" (Truth, 1851). I contend Black women sacrifice some aspect of their well-being to maintain this position. Kesho Yvonne Scott (1991) appears to offer evidence of this in the following recalled memory.

> *"Striding down Greenfield Avenue and across the Southfield Expressway with me crying and following behind, she taught me that my feelings did not matter, that no matter how hurt I was, how ashamed, or how surprised I was, I had to fight back because if I did not, then I would always be somebody's victim. She also taught me a lesson I did not want to learn: she taught me exactly when my private pain had to become a public event that must be dealt with in a public manner. That day my mother offered me no personal comfort for my momentary shame and embarrassment; instead she made me see my pain as not mine. Though she spoke no words directly, she made me realize instinctively that my experience ... was directly related to facts I could not control – my blackness and my womanness" (1991, p. 2).*

Scott's pain of embarrassment or shame is compounded by her mother's emotional detachment. Scott's mother focused her attention on regaining her daughter's dignity versus comforting her in this traumatic moment. In the midst of physical, verbal or emotional abuse, Black girls are taught to suppress their feelings, to "stay strong" and fight back.

Green-Fareed (2006) cites Harris's (2001) assertion of the lasting image of Black women as "either nurturers (saints), tyrants (sinners), or commanders (saviors)." The prevailing image that feeds the SBW perception and syndrome is nurturer: " ... this enduring thread of nurturers to the world, runs through almost every aspect of strong Black women's lives and is most likely the strongest thread impacting our health and wellness" (Green-Fareed, 2006). In my experience, valuing dignity over emotional expression is typical behavior for Black women in the United States and is a two-edged sword. I think both the mother and daughter lost something in this situation in the midst of teaching/learning this lesson.

Inherent in this discussion of 'strong Black womanhood' is the characteristic of resistance. During enslavement, Black mothers taught their daughters to fight back in small, significant ways. In the movie *Amistad,* there is a scene on the ship where the Africans are brought on deck. Those that have died are loosed from their shackles and tossed overboard. A young mother holding her baby is watching this scene. In that moment, she decides she'd rather die than have her fate decided by others. She deliberately and slowly lifts herself and the babe overboard and into the sea.

Yet another trait is resilience. The fact that Black women survived all that we have is a testament to our strength of spirit, as indicated in Brent (1973), Collins (2000), Jones & Shorter-Gooden (2003), Scott (1991) and others. Kesho Yvonne Scott's book, *The Habit of Surviving,* speaks to the fact the Black women are intentional about persisting and moving through, no matter what. Noted poet and author Maya Angelou penned *Still I Rise,* a work I believe embodies the survivalist spirit of Black women. The opening line states, "You may write me down in history with your bitter, twisted lies, you may trod me in the very dirt but still, like dust, I rise" (Angelou, 1994, p. 163).

Conceptual Framework

> *"Scholarly writing about African American women clearly reveals their perilous social position in society because of the interlocking and interactive forces of race, sex and class."*
>
> *Bell and Nkomo, 1998:285*

There is a dearth of research on Black women's development in the field of psychology. Belenky, Clinchy, Goldberger, and Tarule, (1997) produced work early on that examined women's consciousness and defined women's development as different from that of men. Participants represented women of varied ages, races, socio-economic classes and occupations. Gilligan (1993) discussed women's identity formation and their moral development in the context of three studies that revealed their exclusion from psychological research. Neither Belenky (1997) nor Gilligan's (1993) research studies provide targeted insight to the development of Black women in this society.

Gurira (2001) stresses psychology must look to other fields for wisdom about Black women. The small body of research on this group indicates they experience specific psychological wounds. Thomas (2004) points to mainstream psychology's neglect of Black womanhood and overlooking critical aspects in both theoretical and empirical analyses.

> *"If psychology is indeed the science of behavior (and not just the behavior of some), the neglect of study of certain segments of the population, such as Black women, results in missing bricks of foundational knowledge that yield a psychological knowledge base that is faulty, inadequate, and incomplete"*
>
> *(Thomas, 2004, p. 287)*

In addition, the women's movement is not totally inclusive of Black women. In its early beginnings, the rush to embrace Black women into the struggle of feminist issues required they [Black women] subjugate race as an issue, in favor of gender.

> *"[Susan] Faludi's work erases any focus on the way in which race is a factor determining degrees of backlash. That she could completely ignore the specificity of race, and once again construct women as a monolithic group whose common experiences are more important than our differences, heralds the acceptance of an erasure within the realms of popular feminist books – works written to reach mass audiences – of all the work black women and women of color have done (in conjunction with white allies in struggle) to demand recognition of the specificity of race"*
>
> *(hooks, 1993, p. 2).*

The triangle of race, gender and class is a social dynamic critical to understanding Black women in the United States. White men never have to consider this triple identity factor. White women have to navigate gender oppression with the privilege of white skin; Black men navigate race oppression with the privilege of gender. Black women navigate race, gender and class on a daily basis. It is impossible for the Black woman to separate herself from her race, her gender or her class.

Thirteen years have passed since author bell hooks took Black and White women to task for the lack of significant research on Black women's experience, but the problem persists. What research there is exists *outside* the field of human development, spread across numerous disciplines. Black feminists have contributed the greatest depth of work in this area. Only a handful of psychologists have integrated this perspective into their work (Thomas, 2004).

Collins (2000) suggests the Black woman can become empowered by understanding her everyday life. Such consciousness may stimulate her to embark on a path of personal freedom, even if it exists initially primarily in her mind" (p. x). This study will intentionally engage Black women as co-examiners to define and name their own experience for themselves. I expect, in part, for the study participants to experience the empowerment Collins describes.

The facilitator of my CORO *Women in Leadership* training experience would open each session by asking us, "What is it that you don't know that you don't know?" I've chosen to view the study through the lens of critical social theory to answer that question for this research. The results of this study will answer this unspoken question for my co-researchers and will compel me to question what I think *I already know* about race, gender and class oppression as a Black woman.

Social justice activists theorize that one must be aware to be accountable. If you don't know what you don't know, you are not accountable. Once you know what you didn't know, you are wholly accountable for making a conscious decision to change, or to continue from a place of feigned ignorance. The voices of the women who participate in this study provide the context for gaining insight into their lived experience. The framing question "what do you know that you didn't know?" allows study participants to consider their learning from this space of self-examination and determine how best to use the new knowledge. We have two options: continue to carry our pain or decide to release it. The latter will help us determine how we teach future generations of Black girls to navigate these areas differently.

The social group Black girls/women holds my interest for current and future research. This is the group that owns my heart and for whom I would like the world to be different. It is also my intent to add to the research on human development in the field of Black women's psychology.

Researcher's Assumptions

The researcher approaches this study with two primary assumptions because of the previously conducted pilot study. She and her co-researchers will revisit emotional situations or experience painful feelings because of the memory. The researcher further assumes participants will be willing to share their experiences through collective memory work in a collaborative study with other women they may or may not know personally.

Organization of the Study

This dissertation will consist of five chapters. Chapter 1 includes an Introduction, statement of the problem, significance of the study, conceptual framework, and researcher's assumptions.

Chapter 2 is a review of the literature examining Black feminist thought, socioeconomic class, institutionalized oppression, internalized oppression, development of identity, and the psychology of Black women.

Chapter 3 will outline the necessity for using a qualitative study, research method of collective memory work, study participants, data collection and reflexivity of the researcher.

Chapter 4 is a discussion of the pilot study, presentation of the full study research findings with analysis, interpretation and discussions. The chapter will also present a summary of the emergent themes from the data.

Chapter 5 will discuss the socialization process for Black women born and raised in the United States.

Chapter 2: Review of Related Literature

> *"As a society, we know very little about the psychology of Black women, a group of 19 million people – 7 percent of the US population. The way they experience the workplace, the complexities of their romantic lives, the challenges they face as mothers and grandmothers, their spiritual and religious practices, these and so many other aspects of their lives are largely unknown to the wider community."*
>
> *(Jones & Shorter-Gooden, 2003, p. 2)*

This study will focus on describing and understanding how racism, sexism and classism influence Black girls becoming Black women in U.S. society. Race awareness develops in the context of the dominant society; the Black girl's awareness of her race awakens through opportunities for social interaction outside her community of culture. Gender realization likely happens in the family through acculturation in how girls "should" behave. Class awareness occurs when she is old enough to recognize "the haves and the have not's" in her world. I propose each area of realization results in a paradigm shift that colors her ensuing life experiences.

My research focus is Black women born and raised in the United States. I believe our history of forced enslavement and continued oppression in this society created a different socialization experience from that of Black women raised outside the United States. Like many

Black women, I operate in a range of roles at any given time, from daughter to employee. I also belong to a variety of identity groups. Of all these groups my race, gender and class exert the most influence on how I move/have access to move through this society. The first two identities I neither control nor dictate; the third is a condition of socialization and the access that money sometimes provides. They are all blessings/accidents of birth as I am situated in this society.

The aforementioned *Full Text of the Willie Lynch Writings* presents a prescription for controlling the Black female slave and keeping her in a "frozen independent state." The document states that if taught well, generations of Black women would pass the lesson of "independence" on to their daughters. Had I absorbed this lesson at age ten? If so, how did that lesson inform the woman I grew to be? For me, achieving that answer is the crux of this study.

Two primary sources speak to my research question. The first is *Shifting: the Double Lives of Black Women in America* by Charisse Jones and Kumea Shorter-Gooden (2003) and the second is entitled *The Habit of Surviving: Black Women's Strategies for Life* by Kesho Yvonne Scott (1991). The former speaks to Black women's experiences of "shifting" in their day-to-day interactions. The authors collected data through surveys and in-depth interviews with 399 Black women across the United States. They discovered that Black women "shift" as they move from their Black world into the White world, and "shift" again when they move from the White world back into their Black world. This shifting behavior occurs in both Black and White communities as the women navigate and negotiate intersections of race and gender and areas of discrimination. The women in the study were trying to appease White friends and colleagues, or Black friends and significant others. They shifted to accommodate differences in class as well as race and gender.

Scott's (1991) work is a study of Black women living in America in the context of race, gender and class. The author sought to determine what enabled Black women to "survive" across centuries of oppression within the "dominant/mainstream/hegemonic" culture.

She examines the everyday politics of Black women's lives, the origins of Black women scholars' perspectives and activities, and "the social and ideological problems specific to the lives of women of color" (1991, p. 3).

The author uses the phrase "habits of survival" in reference to the external and internal adjustments Black women make to accommodate economic exploitation as well as racial and gender-related oppression. Using life history as her methodology, Scott engaged four women between the ages of forty-six and fifty-two in a collaborative study with her to explore these survival strategies. She interviews her mother separately and engages her nine and eleven year-old daughters to find out what survival strategies they'd learned from her, thus far. Scott noted "the habit of surviving surfaces in the workplace, in schools, and in Black women's liberation movements. Each woman I interviewed used her individual habits as tools to meet head on race and gender discrimination and poverty she encountered" (1991, p. 147).

Black Feminist Theory

> *"This dialect of oppression and activism, the tension between the suppression of African American women's ideas and our intellectual activism in the face of that suppression constitutes the politics of US Black feminist thought"*
>
> *(Collins, 2000, p. 3).*

Patricia Hill Collins (2000) wrote what is considered the landmark text on Black feminist theory entitled, *Black Feminist Thought*. The discipline examines the marginalization of Black women at the intersection of multiple oppressions. Collins posits similarities between Black feminist thought and critical social theory for African American women because both "encompass bodies of knowledge and sets of institutional practices" (p. 9) that consider Black women as a collective body. Black feminist thought and critical social theory both hold a commitment to justice for all oppressed groups (p. 9). Hooks (1989) supports Collins's assertion that Black women are oppressed systemically through economic exploitation, political suppression and educational disenfranchisement.

> *"As a group, black women are in an unusual position in this society, for not only are we collectively at the bottom of the occupational ladder, but our overall social status is lower than that of any other group. Occupying such a position, we bear the brunt of sexist, racist and classist oppression" (1989, p. 16).*

The discipline of Black feminist thought is situated in the intellectual writings of the academy. It exists in the lived experience of Black women elders. Black women who question the status quo, who share their learning from oppression and encourage others to action comprise this group. Contributors to Black feminist theory expand beyond the academy to include Black women from the arts and the community. Collins (2000) considers Sojourner Truth, Bessie Smith and Ma Rainey to be early Black feminists because of their messages, their varied modes of communication, and their appeal to the working class.

The study of lived experience seems central to research on internalized oppression because it is in the living that oppression is experienced, questioned and where resistant action takes place. The women who participated in the pilot study for my research project received diminishing treatment from White people who seemed to believe the cultural ideology that they (White people) were superior. Contributing their lived experiences to this research allows them to participate in the stratum of Black feminist thought. Both Collins (2000) and Thomas (2004) support this assertion. "Because clarifying Black women's experiences and ideas lies at the core of Black feminist thought, interpreting them requires collaborative leadership among those who participate in the diverse forms that Black women's communities now take" (2000, p. 16).

> *"The shared racial and gender background of the Black female researcher and Black female study participant also increases the researcher's ability to engage the participant in authentic ways and to better understand the sociocultural, individual, and other nuance factors that influence the behaviors observed" (Thomas, 2004, p. 301).*

My co-researchers in this study will add to the literature on Black feminist thought by sharing their life experience in collaborative examination.

Socioeconomic Class

> *"Let our girls possess whatever amiable qualities of soul they may ... it is impossible for scarce an individual of them to rise above the condition of servants – Maria Stewart" (Collins, 2000, p. 46)*

Hooks (2000) reminds us that racist biases shaped US history, eliminating information about African explorers and immigrants who preceded Columbus's arrival in this country. These people were never enslaved. The explorers came here bringing gifts of cotton seed and a small number of immigrants came seeking the same freedom as their white counterparts (2000, p. 89). US history relegates Africans' arrival to the 1600s when the first enslaved peoples were brought to these shores (C. Harris & Neal, 2002). This history includes the caste and class divisions that existed among Black people.

The class division present during enslavement was often facilitated by light versus dark skin tone, which often dictated job status on the plantations.

> *"The masters of the more aristocratic plantations, especially in the Sea Island cotton, rice and sugar districts, encouraged*

> *pride of caste in their house servants. Undoubtedly, they sometimes succeeded, and when they did, a sharp social line arose between the slaves of the Big House and those of the quarters. Mary Colquitt of Georgia recalled that her mother, a cook, forbade her to play with the children of the field slaves. According to a member of the mighty Heyward family, the house slaves on their huge estates lived apart from the field slaves and associated with them little"*
>
> *(Genovese, 1976, p. 329).*

Continued class division was often reinforced by employment opportunities, or lack thereof, post-enslavement.

> *"After a quarter of a century of "freedom," vast numbers of Black women were still working in the fields. Those who had made it into the "big house' found the door toward new opportunities sealed shut – unless they preferred, for example, to wash clothes at home for a medley of white families as opposed to performing a medley of household chores for a single white family"*
>
> *(Davis, 1981, p. 88).*

Collins (2000) uses the term "alienated labor" in reference to Black women in the workforce. She states that alienated labor can be paid – domestics, dishwashers, cooks, drycleaning and health care assistants, and professionals engaged in what she calls "corporate mammy work", that is office administration and human resources; or unpaid, i.e., never ending chores of Black grandmothers and single mothers. Her discussion of Black class oppression and women takes place in the context of slavery. Specifically, the discussion focuses on the pre-enslavement, enslavement and post-enslavement periods.

Prior to enslavement, women in West Africa typically combined "work" with family duties centered on motherhood. Childcare involved introducing children to the family business of selling produce in the market and accompanying their mother to harvest crops. When old enough, children assumed responsibilities that supported the family, i.e., caring for siblings, running errands, and generally helping. "Working did not detract from West African women's mothering. Instead, being economically productive and contributing to the family-based economy was an integral part of motherhood" (2000, p. 49).

Enslavement facilitated a forced, paradigmatic shift in Black women's roles at home and at work. Instead of working on behalf of her family, her work efforts benefited the owner of the plantation. He had power and control over the work she performed and the children she produced. "The nature of work performed was altered; their forced incorporation into a capitalist political economy meant West African women became economically exploited, politically powerless units of labor" (2000, pp. 49-50). The Black woman in slavery had no control over her work and no guarantee that she would actually raise her own children.

According to Collins, Black women were forced to work in the fields or as domestics to support their families, post-enslavement. Legalized segregation denied economic parity in housing, education, employment and public accommodations. In this period, "the vast majority of Blacks were poor or working class" (2000, p. 55). African Americans, as a group, were separated by employment opportunities. Women took low-paying, steady work as domestics; men found erratic employment in low-skilled manufacturing jobs that paid well.

What Collins (2000) identifies as Black "civil society" emerged during post-enslavement as African-Americans sought intentionally to hold onto interpersonal relations fostered during enslavement. Following World War II stratification of social class became apparent in the Black community. The working class moved upward creating a fledgling middle class (2000, p. 59). Cushner, McClelland, & Safford (2003) define social class as the process used to distinguish one individual or group from another by assigning "worth" (p. 389). The authors assert that social class refers to a hierarchical stratification of "layering" people in social groups, communities, and societies.

Cushner et al ascribe this tendency to group people according to worth as a human trait. I agree with the authors' assessment of class status and human tendency to flaunt one's advantage at the expense of others. According to NCCJ, 80% of the US population owns only 6% of the nation's wealth.[2] Cushner et al delineate social class categories in the United States as:

- Upper, social elite - generally have inherited social privilege
- Upper middle class -professionals, corporate managers, leading scientists; benefit from extensive higher education
- Lower middle class - small businesses, teachers, social workers, nurses, clerical; desire to belong and be respectable, value friendliness, keeping up appearances
- Working class - largely blue collar workers; struggle with dirtier work, long hours
- Lower class - working poor, underclass (2003, p. 390)

"While many Americans would identify class membership in terms of income, it is important to understand that social class standing depends on a combination of prestige, power, influence, and income" (p. 390).

It is important to remember this demarcation because Collins (2000) asserts that Blacks who lost jobs and couldn't secure re-employment added to the existing population of poor Blacks, thereby increasing the Black underclass. This would translate to the "lower class" category referenced in Cushner et al's categorization. The Black community saw itself as extensions of each other, "equating family with extended family, [and] treating community as family" (2000, p. 55), hence the notion of "the village"[3]. Lips (1999), offers further clarification specific to Black women and class stratification.

2 Source: *Building an Inclusive Community Workshop* "Fabric of Oppression" lecture

3 Black women forced into the workforce left their children in the care of Black women elders and those who could afford to stay at home. These women watched over other women's children as if they were their own, realizing the African proverb "it takes a village to raise a child."

> *"According to the US Bureau of Labor Statistics women make up two-thirds of all minimum wage-earners, and during 1998 women in the United States earned 76 cents for every dollar earned by men. At the managerial level, the wage gap is greater and most noticeable for women of color. At this level, white women earned 74 cents for every dollar earned by men, Asian-American women earned 67 cents, African-American women earned 58 cents, and Hispanic women earned 48 cents (Catalyst, 1997)"*
>
> *(Lips, 1999, p. 2).*

Davis (1989) asserts that Black women's desperate economic situation did not show signs of change until the outbreak of World War II (p.98). At that time, since about sixteen percent still worked in the fields, scarcely one out of ten had really begun to escape the old grip of slavery. Even those who were able to enter industry and professional work were consigned by rule to the worst-paid jobs in these occupations. Consistent with the Bureau of Labor Statistics Women's Pay Equity Report, the salary figure for all women increased by only $0.07 between 1957 and 2000. The works of Collins, Davis, hooks and Lips point up that Black women's place the US economy changed little from enslavement to present day. As the next area of discussion reveals, society is structured to keep the Black woman in this position.

Systems of Oppression

The National Conference for Community & Justice (NCCJ) defines oppression as "the one-way systemic mistreatment of a defined group of people, with that mistreatment reinforced and supported by society" (Cummins et al., 1994). NCCJ further defines racism as "structured inequality whereby white people are the privileged group and people of color are the group targeted by the oppression" (Cummins et al.,

1994, p. 38). Rita Hardiman and Bailey Jackson (1997) conceived the graph below to reflect the "pervasive and systemic hierarchies that hold in place unequal status [members of U.S. society hold] relative to each other" (1997, p. 20). They use the terms 'target' or 'agent' to describe placement of groups in the United States societal system.

> *"Agents are defined as members of dominant social groups privileged by birth or acquisition who knowingly or unknowingly exploit and reap unfair advantage over members of target groups.*
>
> *Targets are defined as members of social identity groups that are disenfranchised, exploited, and victimized in a variety of ways by the oppressor and the oppressor's system or institutions. They are subject to containment, having their choices and movements restricted and limited; are seen and treated as expendable and replaceable, without an individual identity apart from the group; and are compartmentalized into narrowly defined roles"*
>
> *(1997, p. 20).*

TABLE 1. SYSTEM OF OPPRESSION - *Black Women's Position*[4]

Social Group	Agents	Targets
Race and Ethnic	Whites	*People of Color*
Gender	Men	*Women*
Sexual Orientation	Heterosexuals	Gays, Lesbians, Bisexuals
Religion	Christians	Muslims, Jews, Buddhists, etc.
Physical, Psychological Developmental Disability	Able [Bodied] Persons	Disabled Persons
Class	Owning & Middle	*Poor and Working*
Age	Middle/Adult	Young and Elderly

The "System of Oppression" matrix reflects what Hardiman & Jackson consider social group standing within the context of the United States.

a) White men occupy agent status in race, gender and [most often][5] class
b) White women occupy agent status in race and [most often][6] class, and target status in gender
c) Black men occupy the agent status in gender and the target status in race and oftentimes class
d) Black women occupy target status in race, gender and oftentimes class.

Some maintain race and gender are socially constructed, while sexual orientation is biologically defined. Age, physical and mental

4 From *Teaching for Diversity and Social Justice* (p.20), edited by M. Adams, L. A. Bell, P. Griffin, 1997, New York: Routledge. Copyright 1997 by Routledge. Adapted with permission.
5 Brackets mine
6 Ibid

ability are determined by condition of birth, physical evolution or impairment. Still other attributes are inherited or adapted from family orientation: faith affiliation and socio-economic class. Beyond race and gender, target or agent status may be fluid in this system; individuals often occupy multiple positions simultaneously. For example, a middle-aged, Christian, heterosexual, Black woman, raised middle class concurrently holds target and agent status.

The following reflection illustrates how Black women receive these myths as truth, and give them a home in our collective consciousness.

In August 2003, I convened a dialogue series with six Black women as a project for *Healing the Heart of Diversity's* facilitation leadership project. The objective was to see how our experiences mirrored similarities and differences across geographic boundaries. We ranged in age from fifteen to sixty-three and hailed from Canada, New York, Florida, Indiana and South Carolina. Despite geographic, social class and age diversity, we'd received comparable acculturation, shared common experiences, and experienced similar hurts growing up. Each had been labeled "articulate", referred to as "an exception" and called "nigger" at least once by White people. All had been excluded by the upper class and by middle class peers; and four of the six had been the only middle class family in their neighborhoods. We'd all been accused by our Black community of "talking White," questioned about "being Black enough," and contended with the matter of being light skinned or dark skinned.

There was a sense of freedom that we experienced in this micro-lab. We were able to complete each other's sentences; we each freely admitted to walking in the 'never-let-them-see-you-sweat' persona each day. We shared our mutual aversion to being considered "exceptions." We dialogued about the wounds left by racism and sexism. We heaved a collective sigh of relief at being able to remove the masks and "just be," safe in the company of our sisters.

I believe that Black women gravitate towards these occasions to be with one another, to be in company and in connection with each other. Safety is inherent in being surrounded by "the Sisters" and is important for Black women's psychological well being.

> *"Beyond the mask, in the ghetto of the black women's community, in her family, and, more important, in her psyche, is and has always been another world, a world in which she functions – sometimes in sorrow but more often in genuine joy ... – by doing the things that 'normal' black women do"*
>
> *(Collins, 2000, p. 101).*

Collins offers that Black women's sororities, civic and social groups, and faith group affiliations are some of the places where Black women find this harbor. This explains [to me] why I create occasions to commune with other Black women, exclusive of the dominant society. Being in community with other Black women feeds my spirit, I seek out those opportunities wherever I am.

Institutionalized Oppression

The National Conference for Community and Justice (NCCJ) defines institutionalized oppression as:

> *"The system of explicit and tacit rules which supports oppression and which manifests itself through social institutions: education, workforce, government, religion, the community. [It is the] structure which supports a racist society by systematically perpetuating and reinforcing the power of the dominant group over all others" (Tom Cummins et al., 1996)*

While NCCJ's definition is specific to race, the system of oppression categorizes dominance and subordinance by ability, age, appearance, gender, race, religion, sexual orientation and socio-economic class. The system was established during the country's formative years. "In the British colonial empire, English feelings of cultural superiority and racism were used to justify economic exploitation and expropriation of lands. North America acted as a hothouse for the growth of white racism and cultural chauvinism" (Spring, 2004, p. 6).

Althusser (1971) argues that we subjugate ourselves to an ideology, which commands us to subjugate ourselves to existent stereotypes. These beliefs are created and sustained by what he calls *ideological state apparatus (ISA).* Each apparatus functions "massively and predominantly by ideology, but they also function secondarily by repression" (1971, p. 145). The ISAs provide reinforcement of patterned roles and societal beliefs, in perpetuity. Any deviation from these patterns meets with negative feedback from the apparatus structure, and individuals in society.

Societal institutions used to support oppressive ideologies include *the family, religion, government, media, the legal, educational and political systems, and language.* Althusser calls these institutions the *ideological state apparatuses* that work to maintain the systems of oppression. In this context, the Black girl born and raised in the United States evolves in a society where her role is predetermined by ideological state apparatuses. Her "becoming" happens with assistance from these various apparatuses and is reinforced through interactional interfaces in the different apparatus. Each interaction constitutes a re-construction of self as she navigates her lifeworld. What exactly occurs in this construction is unknown. That is the focus of this study.

Internalized Oppression

> *"White you're alright; yellow, you're mellow; brown, stick around; black, get back; red, you're dead."*
>
> *Author unknown*

In her seminal text, Suzanne Lipsky (1987) defines "internalized oppression" as "the turning upon our selves, upon our families, and upon our own people the distress patterns that result from the racism and oppression of the majority society" (1987, p. 4). Jones & Shorter-Gooden (2003) write about the damage that internalized oppression causes to our inner psyche in *Shifting: the Double Lives of Black Women in America*. They cite myths that have become entrenched in society over time.

> *"Stereotypes based on race, gender and social class make it hard to trust oneself and to trust others who look or behave like you do. They set confusing parameters on who you think you are, and what you believe you should or can become"*
>
> *(Jones & Shorter-Gooden, 2003, p. 4).*

The rhymed quote above is familiar from my childhood. It reflects diminishing levels of acceptance for people of different skin color. I don't recall ever hearing other people of color recite this saying. As an adult, I've heard this piece recalled by my contemporaries in Carbondale, Illinois, St. Louis, Missouri, and Orlando, Florida. Our universal knowledge of this insidious rhyme demonstrates how internalized oppression permeates this society, and particularly the Black community.

Collins (2000) shares another version of the rhyme:

> *"Now, if you're white, you're all right,*
> *If you're brown, stick around,*
> *But if you're black, Git back! Git back! Git back!"*
>
> *(p.89).*

The message I get from this particular version is one of subjugation and diminishment. In other words, the darker the skin, the further back one moves from access. Collins discusses the quote in the context of the internalized oppression regarding Black women's hair, skin color and standards of beauty. "Prevailing standards of beauty claim that no matter how intelligent, educated, or "beautiful" a Black woman may be, those Black women whose features and skin color are most African must "git back" (2000, p. 89). This is still a major issue of separation in the Black community today. The question is how did internalized oppression start?

I was introduced to the aforementioned *Willie Lynch* letter in 1997, during a Dismantling Racism retreat convened by the National Conference for Community and Justice (NCCJ). It conveyed instructions to plantation owners in Virginia about how to manage their slave populations to sustain "good economics." I was struck by what appeared to be a plan to carry on the oppression of Black people by creating distrust through separation, while facilitating dependence on Whites. The speech concludes, "if [the plan is] used intensely and properly for one year, the slaves themselves will remain perpetually distrustful". For me, this missive offers insight into how the system of oppression was initially instituted against Black people in US society. As Lipsky (1987) states, internalized oppression is the term for how members of the same social group collude with the system of oppression.

According to Lipsky "internalized oppression is the primary means by which Black people have been forced to perpetuate and "agree" to their own oppression" (p. 1). She asserts that since the subjugation of Black people in this country started with enslavement, every Black person in US society has been affected by internalized oppression. Because of "abuse, invalidation, oppression and exploitation" (p.3), every Black person carries the wounds of racism. I believe that once Black people began acting out these patterns, we became adroit at subjugating ourselves. Lipsky concludes that these distress patterns were created as a response to the oppression and racism from the dominant culture; many of these responses to oppression were developed by our Black ancestors to keep us alive (p.3).

Theorists that support Lipsky's premise include Love (1997, 2000), Kwong (2003) and Rhymes (2005). While institutionalized oppression is maintained via ISAs, internalized oppression is often maintained via members of the target group and meted out upon each other. In *The Mis-Education of the Negro*, Carter G. Woodson (1933) expounds on internalized oppression, specifically as it is carried out in the education system.

> *"When a Negro has finished his education in our schools, then, he has been equipped to begin the life of an Americanized or Europeanized white man, but before he steps from the threshold of his alma mater he is told by his teachers that he must go back to his own people. While he is a part of the body politic, he is in addition to this a member of a particular race to which he must restrict himself in all matters social. While being a good American, he must above all things be a "good Negro"; and to perform this definite function he must learn to stay in the "Negro's place"*
>
> *(1933, p. 6).*

While his assertions were made in the late nineteenth century, I contend that internalized oppression still maintains a strong foothold in society, making his message pertinent today.

Lipsky (1987) wrote her article on internalized oppression as a publication of the Re-evaluation Counseling (RC) communities. The work was initially published in *Black Re-emergence*, the RC publication of Black Liberation and Community Development co-counselors. Lipsky's definition is the basis for several discussions of internalized oppression in society. For example, Love (1997) has suggested that, "*Internalized Oppression is a box within ourselves that keeps us stuck in the same place.*" Engaging this study may perhaps be an opportunity to identify ways that Black women might be able to step out of this 'box'.

Development and Identity

> *"I was born before modern science could accurately determine the gender of unborn fetuses, but it didn't take scientific genius to determine my race. My mother was black. My father was black. That meant ... I would be black. So, long before they knew whether I was a boy or a girl, they knew I was black. That to me says it all. I was born into second class citizenry not because of my gender but because of my race."*
>
> *(Williams, 2000, p. 95)*

General Perspectives on Identity

Black girls and women experience the double oppression of racism and sexism because of who they are born to be in the world. So how do Black girls become "black"? Pyant & Yanico (1991) state that "the most popular developmental model of racial identity is that of Cross (1971), who proposed a five-stage sequence in the development of a positive Black identity" (1991, p. 2). Cross's stages include: *pre-encounter*, where identity formation begins with negative or indifferent feelings toward her racial group. In the *encounter* stage, she discards old thinking and constructs a new identity.

During *immersion-emersion,* she immerses herself in all things Afrocentric, feeling positive towards Black and negative towards White cultures. Next, in the *internalization* stage, she develops positive feelings towards Blacks and balanced feelings towards other groups. In the final stage, *internalization-commitment* the individual demonstrates dedication through engagement in community, social, or political activity. Parham (1993) points out that most of the Nigrescence literature describes the progression from attitudes of self-denigration to self-pride in a linear fashion. He offers that one's psychological experiences may stimulate a recycling through a particular stage.

Cross's (1971) model provides framing around race identity, yet it is still not specific to Black girls and women. Clinical psychologist and author Beverly Greene (1990, 1994) asserts that Black girls born and raised in the United States progress through socialization that differs from that of the dominant culture.

> *"Race operates as a powerful social variable that can intensify other social variables, such as class and education (Ladner, 1971). Therefore the history of racism in the United States affects the experience of gender and may intensify the effects of sexism for African American women"*
>
> *(B. Greene, 1994, p. 16).*

Greene says African American mothers are charged with teaching their children mechanisms for mastering racism. They must determine how to warn their children successfully about racial barriers in ways that do not overwhelm the children, without minimizing the challenge these barriers pose (1994, p. 14).

Spencer (1988) asserts that identity formation should be viewed as a process through which children come to know their names, race, sex roles, social class, and the meanings these descriptions have for their lives. These meanings evolve in the context of the child's particular culture (1988, p. 61). She says identification is ascribed to one's "sense of belonging" to an ethnic group, and consciously identifying with a particular racial group. In their study of identity processes for minority children in America, Spencer and Markstrom (1990) say that preferences indicate group pride and function to reinforce self-respect and affirm self-concept (1990, p. 292).

Diane Harris (1992) designed *A Cultural Model for Assessing the Growth and Development of the African American Female*. Her preliminary study was conducted with 54 African American young women; teenagers aged 14-17 years and college students, 19-25 years. College age respondents were students attending a local university representing diverse sociocultural backgrounds. Adolescent respondents were "teenagers from local high schools, primarily from poor families and communities with limited resources and opportunities" (1992, p. 161).

Harris posits three elements to the model. A *sense of belonging* is defined by interdependence or being connected. A *sense of identity* is influenced by self-perception as a child; it broadens to include knowledge of self as a woman, an African American, and as a unique individual. The *sense of control* is the belief that one can control what happens in one's own life, resulting in a feeling of success (p. 160).

I believe the *sense of control* in the context of an oppressive society is crucial to a Black girl's socialization process. Black girls and Black women do not control all aspects of what happens in their own lives.

> *"... white people established a social hierarchy based on race and sex that ranked white men first, white women second, though sometimes equal to black men, who are ranked third, and black women last"*
>
> *(hooks, 1981, p. 52).*

I consider the following classroom exchange an example of that hierarchical thinking. While giving a guest lecture on inclusion to a diverse class of undergraduate students, I posed this question to White members of the student audience, "How often do you think about being White?" After moments of uncomfortable silence a young White man responded, "That has nothing to do with this topic!" I still find this statement incredible considering the focus of my talk, yet I understand his frame of reference.

In my experience, if the world is set up to accommodate people like you (White, male), then the rhythm of the world flows when *you initiate movement.* There is never a need for you to think about your race or gender, and how these influence your existence. However if you are one of those forced to move in others' flow (Black, female), these same rhythms *wreak havoc upon your existence* as you constantly work to maintain balance in the wake of societal waves (Edwards, 2005)Race,

Class, Gender</keyword></keywords><dates><year>2005</year></dates><publisher>Fielding Graduate University </publisher><work-type>knowledge assessment</work-type><urls></urls></record></Cite></EndNote>. I contend that this relates to one's *sense of control*, or lack thereof. I believe Black girls and women are able to exercise a sense of control over *some* aspects of their lives; I will explore this later.

Bell and Nkomo's (1998) work on "armoring" to withstand racism and oppression relates to Harris' model. They talk about a *sense of belonging* relative to families giving nurturing support, and guiding their daughters in how to adapt and function effectively outside their communities of culture. The authors say *sense of identity* develops when parents involve a daughter in activities that reinforce her self-image and afford her experiences that increase her confidence, enhance her social skills and give her courage to "move comfortably back and forth between two cultural contexts" (p. 288). A *sense of control* is built when Black women learn the ethic of "being strong to the point of becoming invincible" (p. 289).

Like Harris, Wilson (1978) describes the notion of *belonging* relative to Black children. "The person whose attitudes and behavior are congruent with his [her] group expectations tends to develop and maintain a feeling of oneness and belongingness with his [her] group and shares with the other group members a "group consciousness" (p.160). This "group consciousness" is evident as culture provides connection for Black women across geographic, class and age boundaries. Harris's model will help to frame identity formation for Black women as it aligns with gender development.

Shorter-Gooden and Washington (1996) looked at the ego-identity of late adolescent African American women. Study participants were seventeen African American females aged 18-22 who were students at a Southern California community college; many were members of the Black Student Alliance. The authors investigated the extent of racial and gender identity that are core components of identity, and how they are dealt with in identity formation. They also were interested to verify the identity domains – race, gender, sexual orientation, relationships, career, religious beliefs, and political beliefs – that are most salient, and the quality of investment in these domains. Finally, the authors looked at how late adolescent African-American women characterize and portray their identity (1996, pp. 467-468).

They found that race was a source of self-definition more than any other aspect of identity. The women in the study seemed to have positive feelings about being Black. The authors conclude that "while societal context of racism may contribute to the salience of racial identity, it does not automatically mean that the resultant identity will mirror societal views, and thus be negative" (1996, p. 471). Shorter-Gooden & Washington note that while gender was deemed important for all study participants, their limited comments and concurrent discussion of gender along with racial identity suggests the participants saw it as less salient than issues of race (1996, p. 471). The authors note Giddings (1984) conclusion that active work around gender issues is less important than work around racial issues for African-American women. Giddings concluded, and Shorter-Gooden and Washington agreed, that racial issues might demand more attention from Black women for reasons of survival; exploring gender issues doesn't carry this same critical importance for Black women's lives (1984, p. 299).

Harris's (1992) *sense of belonging* relates here where the study shows that relationships were an important part of the women's identities. "Almost all the relationships that helped define their lives were with other women" (Shorter-Gooden & Washington, 1996, p. 472). The authors assert that this finding concurs with "research on women that stresses the importance of connection, in contrast to separation, in their development (Miller, 1991). The developing literature on the importance of a sense of communion or relatedness in people of African origin also helps make sense of this finding" (1996, p. 472). This also supports Collins (2000) notion that "Black women gravitate towards those collective opportunities to be with one another; to be in company and in connection with each other" (2000, p. 101).

Connection, communion and control are important to identity formation and socialization for Black girls growing up in the United

States. Theorists agree that their identity development requires three elements: sense of belonging, sense of identity and sense of control. A study conducted with Black college females indicates that race is the most salient aspect of their identity(Shorter-Gooden & Washington, 1996). The study also concluded that racism does not result in negative self-image for Black girls. They also determined that race and gender are inseparable social constructs.

Social Construction of Self

Guidano (1991) posits that the subjective self (I), and the objective self (Me), are continually interacting in relation to self and in relation to others. The individual is a product of her self-perception. Her knowledge of self constitutes her reality as she sees the world and her self *in* the world. She imitates the behaviors and attitudes of early attachments (parents) to determine how to be in the world. In the process of this imitation, she also "creates a single, subjectively coherent personal identity" (1991, p. 33).

Butler (1990) asserts that gender is comprised of "constructed identity" that evolves over time through repetition of assigned acts. "The act that one does, the act that one performs, is in a sense an act that has been going on before one arrived on the scene" (p. 277). She is in concert with de Beauvoir's notion that a woman "becomes" in the context of conforming to the *idea* of 'woman'. Thereby, gender is constructed and performed, according to a preexisting ideal of what 'woman' is supposed to be. She concludes that since gender is not a fact and expresses no "essence", it is a "construction that regularly conceals its genesis" (p. 273). According to Michael Omi & Howard Winant (1994), this is also true of race; Sennett and Cobb (1973) and Bowles and Gintis (1976) assert the same is true of identity issues related to class.

Okazawa-Rey (2003), states that the identity development process for US born Black women is socially constructed via interactional interface at three levels: *individual, group and society*. She refers to these three levels of identity formation as *micro, meso and macro* (2003, p. 62) in the figure below. At the *individual* level, her early childhood attachment figures provide the first model of who she is and how she should behave (Guidano, 1991, p. 33). Her development is continually constructed in the context of peers and familiars outside of her family. "At this level we define ourselves and structure our daily activities according to our own preferences. We can best feel and experience the process of identity formation, which includes naming specific forces and events that shape our identities" (2003, p. 63).

Figure 1. Ideological State Apparatus, Interactional Interface and Identity Development[7]

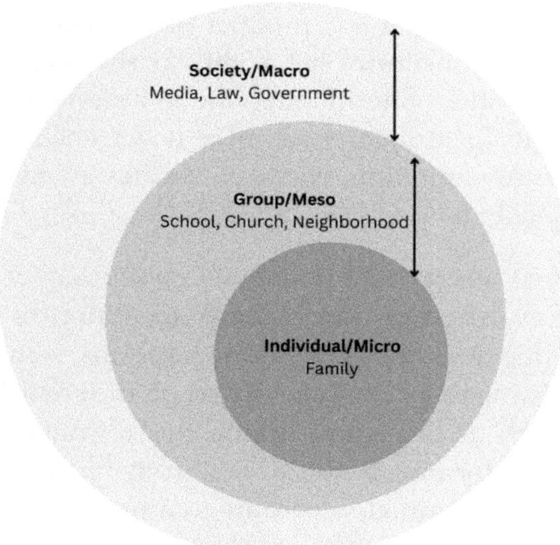

The questions of "Who am I? Who do I want to be? Who do others think I am and want me to be?" (2003, p. 61) evolve in the context of the child's attachment figures through regular interactional interfaces. All this contributes to an "ongoing formulation of self,

7 This figure illustrates the interactional interface that occur at the micro, meso and macro levels, the placement of ISAs, and their influence at various levels of identity development. Copyright R.D. Edwards.

whether or not the process is conscious, deliberate, reflective, or even voluntary" (2003, p. 63). Who we are and who we become in the world is determined by our responses to the people in the environments around us; individual choice has very little to do with this formation (M. Okazawa-Rey, 2003). One could easily overlay Harris's (1992) three elements over this interface: sense of belonging happens in the individual sphere; sense of identity evolves at the group area; and sense of control is flexed in the societal field. To me, this is where sense of control might be challenged and Black women may experience decreased control.

At the *group* level, the Black girl experiences more interaction with those external to the nuclear family. Guidano (1987) posits that she stops mimicking attitudes and behaviors of earlier attachments and begins to form her own attitudes in concert with and as mirrored by her peers. The self is now constructed in relation to interactions with her social connections. This includes non-nuclear family members, friends, and teachers. Guidano's framing, along with Kirk & Okazawa-Rey's (2003) interactional interface reinforce Parham, White and Adjisa's (2000) assertion that Black people learn to view themselves based on what they are told about their place in the world, who the world says they are, and how they *should*[8] behave in it. These messages come from the other societal institutions that contribute to the construction of her 'self': neighborhood, school, and church, as stated by Collins (2000, p. 86-87).

At the macro/societal level, she engages a broader exchange of ideas. "The single most visible signifier of identity is physical appearance; how we look to others affects their perceptions, judgments, and treatment of us" (Kirk & Okazawa-Rey, 2003, p. 64). Now she interfaces with the enforcing aspects of the *ideological state apparatuses,* government and the media, and the repressive state apparatus, law enforcement (Althusser, 1971). I contend that these apparati are pervasive in their ability to classify and label human beings; these apparati distinguish who is included and excluded, and determine who is assigned status and who has access to power and privilege.

8 Italics are mine.

Black Girls "Becoming" in the Context of Racism, Sexism, and Classism

> *"Little is known about how African-American women weave an identity comprised of attitudes and feelings about themselves as Blacks, as women, and as unique individuals. Moreover, since all of the reviewed studies are quantitative in approach, little is known about how African-American women themselves talk about and depict their identity"*
>
> *(Shorter-Gooden & Washington, 1996, p. 467).*

Niobe Way (1998), in her study of Black and Latino/a, poor and working class boys and girls, interviewed the same select group of students over a three year period. When asked whether they experienced racism and sexism, boys spoke about their direct clashes with racism. Girls in the study primarily responded that they were aware of the reality of racism; yet they indicated lack of or infrequent brushes with direct experiences of racism (1998, pp. 205-206). Black girls in the study spoke of expecting to encounter racism and being prepared to "transform other people's opinions" (p. 214) as a way of mitigating the encounter when it occurred. They also spoke of not using their blackness as an excuse.

> *"I'm proud to be black and everything. But I know, I'm aware of racist acts and racist things that are happening in the world. But I use that as no excuse, you know. I feel as though I can succeed.... That's no excuse being black. In fact, I think that being black is good. I'm proud to be black but you also gotta face reality and what's going on, you know. Black people are not really getting anywhere in life. But I know I will....I just know I will. Well, I'm determined to. I mean if someone else up there who's hiring isn't willing to help, what can you do? You know? But it's not an excuse, but you gotta do – sometimes you gotta do what it takes to*

survive" Eva, African American girl

(1998, p. 214).

Way (1998) puts forward that while the girls may not directly experience racism, they do encounter the subtle oppression that comes in the form of negative stereotyping, i.e., "they get pregnant", "they're all on welfare". Even if they claim that they have never directly experienced discrimination, these girls are actively responding to the stereotypes as they aspire to be successful (1998, p. 221). I find it sad that these young Black girls appear to be armoring themselves in anticipation of racist experiences. Even more distressing is the fact that negative stereotypes about them are such a part of their socialization, that they don't recognize stereotypes as racist, sexist or classist aspects of diminishment. This behavior is in concert with the sense of control put forward by Harris (1992) and Bell & Nkomo (1998). The positive in this is their resistant attitude towards stereotypes and their prepared resilience for the racist encounter they have been socialized to anticipate.

Pastor, McCormick and Fine (1996) speak to this sense of resistance in research they conducted with five adolescents – two high school and three middle school girls – from working class neighborhoods in New York City. The research took place during a summer and comprised of the young women's narratives, research-participant group discussions, and ethnographic observations at the girls' school sites. The girls were Jewish American, European-Latina American, Dominican Latina, African American and Caribbean-African (1996, p. 17).

> *"Women often begin a lifetime of resistance as social individuals working to influence the interactions that take place in their homes, schools, and communities. The sense of agency that results from resisting oppressive structures influences who we are as women – our identity – and this identity formation process begins in our youth"*

(Pastor et al., 1996, p. 19).

The authors contend that these urban girls are unstoppable in their desires to preserve and develop their personal integrity while resisting the offensive boundaries constructed against them because of their race, gender, class or culture (1996, p. 26). It's my interpretation that the spaces where these girls live and navigate society cultivate in them individual pools of resistance. Dominican Marina fights sexist oppression in her home where her father and brothers receive privileged treatment. Sixteen-year old Nikki, an African American, finds voice in her poetry, refuting both the failure of her high school to provide her with a sound education and the loss of connection to her home. Tanzania, also African American, uses her words to critique the disparate images that the White media projects about her community. The authors acknowledge Tanzania's "uncanny ability to *deconstruct*, critically, the messages floating in the culture about gender, race, sexuality, and class" (1996, p. 27), as evidenced in the following poem.

> *"Don't hurt me anymore; don't follow me like the rapist stalks his prey. Don't quiet the words I have to say like a rapist covers the mouth of his victim to hold back what she must say.*
>
> *Don't rip savagely apart my dreams as a rapist rips the clothes off his victim; don't throw me down when I try to get up like a rapist throws his victim down when she tries to escape.*
>
> *Don't beat me when I struggle to learn and survive; don't pin my thoughts down like a rapist pins the arms of his victim on the cold concrete. Don't heave your hateful thoughts down on me like a rapist heaves his body down on his victim.*
>
> *Don't thrust anymore of your sick ideas into my head like a*

rapist thrusts his body into his screaming victim; don't force me to say what you want like a rapist forces his victim to perform debasing sexual acts.

Don't leave me crying without a shred of confidence to go on without a shred of dignity to continue living. Don't make me second guess myself when I know I have the right to speak. You've left me with the hate I never asked for.

Rapist. Racist. They look almost the same.

Rapist. Racist. They are the same"

(Pastor et al., 1996, p. 27).

Janie Victoria Ward (1996) asserts that Black mothers have learned to skillfully weave lessons of critical consciousness into moments of parent-child intimacy, and to cultivate resistance against societal practices that can erode a Black child's self-confidence and impair her positive identity development (1996, p. 86). She says that Black parents socialize their children from a foundation of cultural and political interpretations and assumptions garnered from their lived experience being Black in White America. She further states that lessons of resistance are those that instruct the black child to determine when, where, and how to resist oppression, as well as to know when, where, and how to accommodate to it (1996, p. 87). Ward interviewed African American adolescent boys and girls and the parents of Black adolescents. Participants voluntarily engaged in private, open-ended, semi-structured interviews to interpret the nature of socialization from their own perspectives.

Mothers and fathers in the study reported sharing with their children stories of prejudice and institutional racism from their past and present experiences. This sharing enabled parents to communicate that "they've been there too and can see what their children see, feel their pain, and share their frustration" (1996, p. 91).

Ward (1996) says this process allows Black parents to convey what Vander Zanden (1989) calls "a psychological sense of oneness" (1996, p. 91) to their children. Ward also cites the American Association of University Women's 1990 report, *Shortchanging Girls, Shortchanging America* as evidence of Black girls' strong sense of self.

> *"Black girls in the study began with and were better able to retain higher levels of self-esteem through adolescence than their white and Latina counterparts. A sense of individual and personal self-worth was important in the structure of self-esteem for black girls. Closeness to family was also central to overall self-esteem, and family and black community reinforcement appeared to sustain high levels of self-esteem (AAUW, 1991, 1992)"*
>
> *(Ward, 1996, p. 88).*

Spencer & Markstrom-Adams (1990) concur with the AAUW when they present Rotherman & Phinney's (1987) ethnic or racial group identity as one's sense of belonging to an ethnic group. They point out that while ethnic identification implies one's ability to define oneself as a member of a certain group, identity indicates *internalization* of identification. I would relate Vander Zanden's sense of oneness to this "sense of belonging" forth by Harris (1992), and defined as interdependence or connectedness. I see this connection as critical to Black girls' understanding of racial and gender oppression. I agree with what the AAUW data suggests; the sense of oneness or belonging provided by parents helps Black girls develop a healthy resistance to cultural pressures.

Yi & Shorter-Gooden (1999), in their treatise on ethnic identity formation, propose a "constructed self over the essentialist notion of the self, which treats self as if it were a substance or an unchangeable essence" (1999, p. 18). The authors consider previous theories on identity development and ethnic identity that presented this maturation in stages. They favor the social constructionist approach which acknowledges one's "becoming" in multiple developmental scenarios where the person has come to craft her unique ethnic self-definition (1999, p. 19). I believe this takes into account individual growth through societal interactions embedded in the context of racism, sexism and classism. These interactions occur within the frame of daily exchanges with family, friends, society and ideological state apparatuses.

Psychology of Black Women

> *"The psychology of Black women is different from that of White women and Black men. Race and gender are inseparable constructs for Black women. In essence, femaleness and Blackness are articulated differently across various contexts of intersecting marginalizations and interlocking identities such that neither gender nor race has independent centrality in the lives of Black women at all times."*
>
> *(Thomas, 2004, p. 287)*

W. E. B. Du Bois (1969) declared "the Negro ... ever feels his two-ness – an American, a Negro; two souls, two thoughts, two unreconciled strivings; two warring ideals in one Black body" (p. 45). Wilson (1978) asserts "this double consciousness" is an existential fact of Black existence and its influence for better or worse, is pervasive in all areas of Black behavior" (p.52). I agree with Du Bois and Wilson and call attention to what both scholars omit – consideration of the Black woman and her unique "three -ness". Because race, gender and class define the Black woman's existence, her evolution occurs in this milieu; she must evolve and develop her psychological consciousness in this social context. She exists in the dailyness of oppression, doing the peculiar dance performed by Black women in US society – what Scott (1991) calls our "cultural chorus line" (p. 8).

Who are we really as Black women in this country? Our presence here spans over three centuries, yet research on this social group in the psychological literature is still wanting. Although my framing is recent, my search began in elementary school as I viewed images in books of people who looked nothing like me. The presentation of Black people only as enslaved persons minimizes their significant contributions to United States culture. Thanks to my mother, I read historic novels about Sojourner Truth, the first notable Black feminist; Phyllis Wheatley, the first published Black poet; Harriet Tubman, the "Moses" of her people; and Ida B. Wells, journalist and anti-lynching crusader in elementary school.

When I started researching this topic in 2002/2003, I would enter search phrases like "black women's psychology" and "human development in black women." I was surprised to get articles focusing on sexual activities of young Black girls or the presence of HIV/AIDS in the Black population, both male and female. I changed "black" to "African American" in hopes of expanding the search: nothing changed. Collins (2000) explains this phenomenon when she discusses "controlling images" (p. 85) of Black women. One of my professors suggested I look in the feminist literature since there really wasn't much written from a scholarly perspective about Black women in traditional psychology. The feminist works revealed more than what I previously found, yet still showed a dearth in the literature (Bell & Nkomo, 1998; Collins, 2000; Davis, 1981; Giddings, 1984, 2001; Gurira, 2001; hooks, 1981, 1993; Jones & Shorter-Gooden, 2003; Pyant, 1991).

The *Journal of Black Psychology* produced a special issue in August 2004 deliberately focused on the psychology of Black women. Psychologist and author Veronica Thomas writes the introduction to the issue and authors the first article. She discusses the lack of psychological literature on Black women in the context of "their multiple identities and oppressions in American society." She also puts forth a definition for this area of the discipline where none existed. "The psychology of Black women is the systemic study of the motivations, cognitions, attitudes, and behaviors of Black women taking into consideration the contextual and interactive effects of history, culture, race, class, gender, and forms of oppression" (2004, p. 290).

In *The Psychology of Black Women: Studying Black Women's Lives in Context*, Thomas discusses the state of scholarly study on the psychology of Black women. She reminds us that the psychology of Black women differs from that of Black men, White women and other non-Black women and supports the notion that race, gender and class are inseparable for Black women (2004, p. 287). Thomas explicates the domain of psychology for Black women. She discusses related conceptual frameworks including Black feminist theory, feminist psychology, and Black psychology; and offers guiding principles as a foundation for future research in this area.

> *"Knowledge Development – work in the psychology of Black women must focus on knowledge development that generates a more profound understanding of Black women (2004, p. 297).*
>
> *Contextuality – Psychological works on Black women must be culturally attached rather than devoid of any meaningful influences outside of the individual psyche (p. 298).*
>
> *Connectedness – The psychology of Black women must promote an approach to studying the lives of Black women that connects this population's motivations, attitudes and behaviors to individual characteristics as well as microfeatures and macrofeatures of the environment (p. 298).*
>
> *Collaboration and Cross-Fertilization – Truly understanding these dynamics, particularly in relation to Black women, must be informed by the insights and scholarship of multiple disciplines such as psychiatry, anthropology, sociology, economics, Black and African studies, women's studies, and health. Only through multidisciplinary perspectives can*

> *the intellectual scope of the psychology of Black women be strengthened (p. 299).*
>
> *Diversity and Equity – The psychology of Black women should foster conceptual and methodological orientations that justly and respectfully view Black women in all their diversity, valuing the enormous strength of this population rather than considering them as a monolithic group with problems that need solving (p. 299).*
>
> *Dissemination – An important principle relates to the promotion of ongoing efforts to disseminate scholarly inquiry from the study of Black women in mainstream and specialized psychology journals and texts, as well as through other forums (e.g., presentations at professional meetings). Too little work is being published in the psychological literature on the lives of Black women (pp. 299-300).*
>
> *Advocacy – Scholarship in the psychology of Black women promotes the interdependence of knowledge and activism. Advocacy should serve as a catalyst to advance work to improve the quality of life for Black women. Scholarship in the psychology of Black women should represent social justice and critical enterprises whereby scholars advocate change and are ever willing to speak out against theories, research paradigms, and social policies that have oppressive effects on the lives of Black women and men (p. 300).*

Finally, Thomas suggests that Black women in the field of psychology are the ones who must conduct research on Black women. Both researcher and research subject share experiences with the multiple oppressions of race, gender and oftentimes class.

The principles set forth by Thomas (2004) are important to this proposed study. The question of how Black girls become Black women is a question about human development that is worthy of further academic research. For the discipline, this study meets the criteria of *knowledge development* as defined by Thomas to generate more profound understanding of Black women (p. 297). Attending to this question in collaborative inquiry with other Black women provides the cultural attachment put forth in Thomas's principle of *contextuality* (p. 298). Exploring the questions "*What is your first memory of being Black?*" "*What is your first memory of being a girl? What is your first memory of having what others didn't and not having what others had?*" allow Black women to identify shared experiences and exhibit Thomas's principle of *connectedness* (p. 298). This is reflected in the women sharing and identifying experiences that link them across age and class boundaries in the context of U.S. culture.

This review of literature confirms the state of interlocking oppressions Black women live under in the United States. It also demonstrates the insufficiency of research done on how Black girls born and raised in the United States become Black women, a significant human development issue for the culture. This need is substantiated by scholars (Bell & Nkomo, 1998; Hoare, 1991; hooks, 1981; Jones & Shorter-Gooden, 2003; Mama, 1995; Reid, 2004; Scott, 1991; Shorter-Gooden, 2004; Thomas, 2004) who conducted studies on differing aspects of the psychology and socialization of Black women. This study will add to the literature on Black women in the United States. In addition, it will elucidate an important aspect of their development in the context of race, gender and class oppression.

This review of literature supports the theory that Black girls in the US exist at the intersection of race, gender and class. Race is a primary means of self-definition for Black girls and Black women. Racism, however, does not result in Black girls having a negative perception of self. Gender is important, yet it does not have the same critical sense of importance to Black girls as race. The review also reveals that Black girls require three essentials to their socialization: sense of belonging, sense of identity and sense of control (Bell & Nkomo, 1998; D. J. Harris, 1992; Spencer, 1988; Wilson, 1978).

The sense of belonging provides relationship, connection and interdependence; it answers the questions, "Who are you?" and "Who are your people?" Sense of identity speaks to sense of self and helps one define self for oneself; it answers the question "Who do I come from?" and supports internalization of identity. The sense of control resolves the question, "Who am I in the face of the world?" I can prepare myself, steel myself, and resolve to release. Sense of control speaks to resistance and resilience; the culture of familiars socializes the Black girl to know when, where and how to resist. This triumvirate of "senses" provides the underpinning of identity formation for Black girls in the United States.

Chapter 3: Design and Methods

"Many Black women in the United States are broken-hearted. They walk around in daily life carrying so much hurt, feeling wasted, yet pretending in every area of their life that everything is under control. It hurts to pretend. It hurts to live with the lies. The time has come for black women to attend to that hurt."

(hooks, 1993, p. 29)

Research Design

This will be a qualitative study using collective memory work as collaborative inquiry to describe, examine and interpret Black women's lived experiences. The research objective is to explore how Black girls develop into Black women in the milieu of a racist, sexist and classist society. Thus, the inquiry will be situated in current research on the psychology of Black women and Black feminist theories. Chapter 3 will outline the necessity for developing a qualitative study, utilizing collective memory work as a form of collaborative inquiry; involving study participants in data collection and interpretation; and engaging the reflexivity of the researcher.

There are two critical facets of this study: whose voice speaks about the lived experiences of Black women, and who conducts the research. The voices of Black women living at the intersection of race, gender and class offer the most accurate view of this reality.

> *"Undoubtedly, it is the case that Black female psychologists are those individuals most likely to express interest and pursue scholarship in the psychology of Black women. In fact, because of Black female psychologists' direct experiences with interlocking identities and multiple oppressions, they are often in a better position to study Black female populations. Black women, in contrast to other groups of psychologists, have histories and experiences that may enable them, as researchers, to develop theory, conduct research, and draw conclusions that are more contextually valid for the life experiences of this population. The shared racial and gender background of the Black female researcher and Black female study participants also increases the researcher's ability to engage the participant in authentic ways and to better understand the sociocultural, individual, and other nuance factors that influence the behaviors observed"*
>
> *(Thomas, 2004, p. 301).*

As participant-observer, I share the same race and gender as my research population. For this reason, I am the logical conduit for examining, interpreting and reporting these occurrences.

Qualitative Research

The purpose of this study is to explore how Black girls become Black women. It is particularly designed to examine and interpret their socialization in the framework of racism, sexism, and classism.

The answer to the question is best given by Black women who live this experience, day-to-day. Qualitative research offers the best avenue for exploring the study question because it is designed to embrace the emotional, psychological, and social complexity of lived human experiences.

A qualitative approach allows the researcher entrée to "attend to that hurt" as hooks (1993) mentions in the opening quote to this chapter. Hooks' assessment of pretense resonates with Harris's (1992) third step of development for African American women – sense of control. This study invites Black women to surface those issues that keep them "walking around in a state of pretense" as hooks claims. It is particularly beneficial that because of shared race and gender, the primary researcher may connect with participants via similarity in life experience. Qualitative and collaborative research permits each woman to function as both subject and researcher in this investigation.

Marshall and Rossman (1999) assert that qualitative methods allow the researcher to engage the study from a naturalistic perspective, interpret the lived experiences of study participants, use a combination of inquiry methods to reflect participants' humanity, recognize and capture emergent data, and consider herself in the research (p.2).

The researcher will explicate these attributes in the study design and implementation.

Collaborative Inquiry

> *"Collaborative inquiry (CI) provides a systematic structure for learning from experience. Participants organize themselves in small groups to address a compelling question that brings the group together. In order to construct new meaning related to their question, collaborative inquirers engage in*

cycles of reflection and action, evoke multiple ways of knowing, and practice validity procedures. "

(Kasl & Yorks, 2002, p. 3)

Collaborative inquiry (CI) is grounded in the theory of a "collective". Each member contributes to the group's learning from her own lived experience. CI comes from the family of experienced or action based methodologies. "Other strategies commonly included in this group are action research, action inquiry, action learning, action science, and participatory action research" (Kasl & Yorks, 2002, p. 3). According to Dodds, (1995), "the method works as a therapeutic tool for all participants" (p. 37) in addition to enabling data collection.

A founding principle of CI is the co-examining of individual lessons to facilitate understanding for all group members (Bush, 2003; Dodds, 1995; Kasl & Yorks, 2002). Smith (2002) indicates when a CI group communicates its experience through public discourse the total group benefits from the empowering value of learning through lived experience (2002, p. 24). The power of mutual learning may strengthen connections among participants. An expected outcome of CI methodologies is action from group members toward change. From this study, the action will be individual as study participants respond differently in their life worlds. I suspect the effects of any changed behaviors have the potential to initiate a ripple effect in their circles of influence with Black girls and other Black women.

Collective Memory Work

"The very notion that our own past experience may offer some insight into the ways in which individuals construct themselves into existing relations, thereby themselves repro-

ducing a social formation, itself contains an implicit argument for a particular methodology."

(Haug, 1987, p. 34)

German feminist scholar Frigga Haug (1987) created Collective Memory Work (CMW) to investigate 'female socialization' – "the process whereby individual women become part of society" (Haug, 1987, p. 33). She believes

"Memories are characterized by contradictions and silences as the 'past-self' engages with the 'present-self'. Contradictions serve the purpose of "non-recognition, denial and repression" of past experiences which memories may invoke, while silence is "another way of coming to terms with the unacceptable"

(Farrar, 2001, p. 2).

According to Haug's design, CMW works with a collective that proceeds through "cycles of reflection" in at least three phases: collection of written memories, collective analysis of the written memories and analysis in the context of scholarly theories (Crawford, Kippax, Onyx, Gault, & Benton, 1992). A copy of the worksheet Haug developed to guide this process is included in *Appendix 1*.

Patricia Farrar (2001) used CMW to study the social construction of women's sexuality in the 1960s. She asserts the process of collectively sharing memories helps research participants to rework their own memory "and find meaning in what may have been either incomprehensible or taken-for-granted" (2001, p. 4). This concurs with the assertions of Bush (2003), Dodds (1995) and Kasl and Yorks (2002) that co-examination is a benefit to all group members. Travis (2003) states,

"Collective memory-work is a social-research method that collapses theory and experience in order that participants gain

> *an understanding. It is a collective way of working with small groups to examine early experiences. The aim of collective memory-work is social change or liberation" (p. 44).*

Co-researchers in this study will use collective memory work (CMW) as a form of collaborative inquiry to undertake the research question. Collective memory work appeals to me as the primary researcher.

One of my goals with this study is that the voices of Black women be heard in defining their own lived experience. The women's voices give the research a phenomenological perspective; each study participant will share her experience with racism, sexism and classism. Our shared ancestry of enslavement coupled with acculturation in survival and independence offers a unique opportunity to name how our socialization occurs. As a social group, Black women have worked collectively against racism and sexism, yet our voices were often unheard and still are frequently overlooked (Giddings, 2001). Haug's research design will give study participants power to name their own experiences.

Research Questions

The objective of this study is to determine how Black girls born and raised in the United States become Black women." Participants will engage the following questions to address this query: What is your first memory of being Black? What is your first memory of being a girl? What is your first memory of having what others did not and not having what others did? The researcher leaves open the option to engage subsequent questions as may be defined with co-researchers in the study.

Definitions

The terms "Black" and "African American" are used in this study to specify Black women born and raised in the United States. This excludes women of shared skin color born outside the United States and currently living here, non-Black women born in Africa and reared or currently residing in the U.S., and women of shared skin color born in the U.S. and reared outside this society.

Participants

The study will be conducted in Orlando, Florida. Following IRB approval, the researcher will make personal contact with five women who are part of an informal and large friendship network. The researcher belongs to that network. The researcher has no working or employment relationship with potential participants. To reduce further the possibility of subtle coercion, the researcher will let potential participants know that there are others who qualify and who have expressed interest in participating in the study. Following this strategy, potential participants should not feel in any way obligated to participate in the study.

The primary researcher will invite five women, aged 21-80, to engage the study questions over the course of six, three-hour sessions using the Collective Memory Work process. Prior to session one, the primary researcher will distribute question one to participants to write their memory, in preparation for the first session. Each person will have an opportunity to respond to the session focus question, in turns. At sessions one, three and five each participant will take turns sharing their written memory, specific to the focus question for that session. Everyone will record their observations on the CMW worksheet and share their insight with the participant via in-session dialogue.

The participant will rewrite the memory at home, incorporating these observations and come prepared to share their rewrite at sessions two, four and six. I will explain these instructions in the letter of invitation and in a one-on-one conversation with invited participants. We will agree on a scheduled time for the debrief session before leaving session six. This debrief will take place approximately one month after the last session of the CMW process.

Screening Criteria

Study participants meet the following criteria:

(1) They are born and raised in the United States
(2) They self-identify as "Black" or "African American"
(3) They are between the ages of 21 and 80
(4) They commit to maintaining confidentiality by signing the *Professional Assistance Confidentiality Agreement* (Appendix 5)

Note: All participants are asked to attend all sessions and the final debrief session; however if someone chooses to leave the study, they will not be replaced.

Data Collection and Analysis

The study will be conducted over six sessions comprised as follows:

- Session I: Conduct participant introductions and orient them to the study. In addition, the primary researcher will:
    - discuss confidentiality and anonymity
    - review the *Informed Consent* form and *Professional Assistance Confidentiality Agreement*, and collect signed documents from participants
    - provide copies of *collective memory work* theory
    - discuss the collective memory work process and tools
    - share resources for dealing with emotional issues

  - discuss audio tape recording and note taking during all sessions, and transcription of recordings by a professional, external to the group

- Sessions 1-6: Participants will engage the study questions (see p. 49) using the collective memory work process. At sessions one, three and five each participant will take turns sharing their written memory, specific to the focus question for that session. Participants will review their memory at home and be prepared to share and discuss any additions or enhancements to the memory at sessions two, four and six.
- Final debriefing session: All participants are encouraged to attend this session to hear the research outputs/themes and to share insights and new learning from their individual experience in this process.

Each of the sessions will be audio-recorded to ensure accurate documenting of the research process. This will also uphold the researcher's intent that the voices of Black women define their own socialization in this study.

A professional transcriptionist, considered part of the research project team, will also sign the *Professional Assistance Confidentiality Agreement* (Appendix 5). At the end of each session, the researcher will send the recording electronically to the transcriptionists, while maintaining the master copy in her home office. Through listening and reviewing the transcripts, the researcher will identify themes from the collective memory work sessions. The themes will be collapsed into a narrative report for review by the participants following the small group inquiry sessions. Participants will be asked to review the transcripts and share their comments via email with the primary researcher. All review comments will be collapsed into one document for discussion during the final participant debriefing session.

Validity and Credibility

Qualitative research requires the investigator to ensure credibility of the study. This is best accomplished through establishing validity. Common procedures used to ascertain validity in qualitative projects include member checking, triangulation, thick description, peer reviews and external audits (Creswell & Miller, 2000). Collective memory work is highly interpretive. This study will employ a multiple lens approach to validity: triangulation to identify themes or categories emergent in the data, engaging the researcher's ability for reflexivity while she reviews the data, and engaging study participants to check the data and confirm the emergent themes. In addition, peer debriefing will take place with faculty and colleagues well versed in qualitative research and the appropriate subject areas brought to bear in the interpretation of the data.

Reflexivity and Role of the Researcher

Reflexivity, the practice of locating self in the research while remaining cognizant of one's impact and influence on the research, is critical to qualitative inquiry. It is particularly important to be mindful of this dynamic in racial and feminist discourse. In this society, I walk a path carved out by Black women who came before me. Like any other situation, it is impossible for me to separate myself from my race, my gender or my life world. Robson, (1989), citing Kirby and McKenna (1989), states:

> *"Remember that who you are has a central place in the research process because you bring your own thoughts, aspirations and feelings, and your own ethnicity, race, class, gender, sexual orientation, occupation, family background, schooling, etc. to your research" (p.49).*

As researcher, it is my responsibility to uphold the guiding principles of "knowledge development, contextuality and connectedness" (Thomas, 2004, p. 297) in carrying out research simultaneously with and on Black women. Occupying a "participant-observer" role in this project, I am constantly aware of my need to remain objective. Separating me from the "participant" aspect of participant-observer is practicable. My experience conducting the pilot study evidences my ability to "let the data come" (Bentz & Shapiro, 1998, p. 102) while also "becoming an object to myself, to be both subject and object" (Callero, 2003, p. 120).

When I started my doctoral program, I instinctively knew I would do research on Black women. My focus became clear as I reflected on my upbringing and recognized the one query I've lived with most of my adult life: "how did we (Black women) get like this?" I hope my approach to this subject, and sensitivity to the research population, develops the reader's understanding of Black women in the context of the United States – of who we are and how we move through society. It is especially important that young and mature Black women have an understanding of our socialization process. Being able to see yourself in the data, to recognize self in the story is important to our psychology and our human development.

Chapter 4: Findings and Discussion

> *"To be a black woman, therefore, is not just to be a Black who happens to be a woman, for one discovers one's sex sometime before one discovers one's racial classification. One discovers what it means to be Black, and all that the term implies, usually outside the family. Until recently, the child had only dim revelations about her color within the family and it was only when she moved out into the community and the opposition and reaction of whites to her gave her insight into her place, racially."*
>
> *(Lindsey, 1970, p. 87)*

The impetus for this study is my curiosity about how Black women in the United States, despite growing up in different parts of the country, appear to share some unity of thought. I think I have personally experienced Frigga Haug's (1987) notion that memory is a social, historical, and political process. We seem to have heard similar stories from our families and learned life lessons from the same old adages. Oftentimes we are able to complete each other's sentences: it's as if we all access the same memory bank. I started to notice this phenomenon while working on my master's degree in Carbondale Illinois. My closest friend was from Vivian, Louisiana and I am from Awendaw, South Carolina. We share a rural upbringing, a very common sense approach to life, and often came to the same conclusions about a situation based on similar life lessons we'd been taught.

After graduation, I moved to St. Louis, Missouri. My Black women friends from professional, personal and faith community circles exhibited this same common sense approach to life and living. Holiday gatherings were multi-generational events and our interactions reminded me of being with my mother and sisters. I currently live in Orlando, Florida where I've developed new Black female friendships. We also share the same memory bank.

When I decided to enter a doctoral program, I knew that my research topic would be Black women. It was essentially a matter of defining the scope of the research and what method to use. Each assessment led me closer to that objective. One faculty member kept telling me to "go deeper" as I fleshed out my research proposal. When I considered research methods, collaborative inquiry resonated with me. It made sense that Black women work together to describe this tendency and it supports Thomas's (2004) principle of "contextuality." The method also matched the culture of inquiry that spoke to my heart – critical social research – for conducting a study on Black women.

Both the pilot and main study offered opportunities for me to use collaborative inquiry. Participants in the pilot were close friends; those in the full study were acquaintances from my professional and faith communities. The method was similar, yet each group had its own diverse characteristics; and if groups could have personalities, I would venture to say each had a distinct one. I was a participant-observer in both study experiences. While the main study group is the focus of the dissertation discussion, the pilot sessions offer some initial insight into early thinking of US born Black women.

The Pilot Study

Pilot research was conducted in an effort to describe and understand how Black girls born and raised in the United States become Black women. Four Black women living in Orlando, Florida participated in this collaborative inquiry. Two were born and raised in Florida: Jacksonville and Gainesville; and two hail from South Carolina: Awendaw and Spartanburg. Participants used the Collective Memory Work (CMW) process *(Appendix 2)* to explore the research question. All participants signed an "*Informed Consent*" *(Appendix 4)* and a "*Professional Assistance Confidentiality Agreement*" *(Appendix 5).*

The primary researcher was a participant in this study. The group ranged in age from mid-thirties to late fifties; two of the women are married, one with children. Three of the four women have master's degrees. One is a juvenile justice social worker for the state of Florida; one is in public relations at DisneyWorld, another is an interior designer and office assistant, and the fourth is coordinator of adult education at a municipal library. Two of the women are friends of the convener and attend the same church; the third is a professional acquaintance.

Each woman understood the purpose of the study and the proposed use of the data. The question we focused on in the pilot study was, *What is your first memory of being Black?* Following CMW protocol, each woman wrote a descriptive narrative of her response to the question. When the group convened, each woman took turns reading her response aloud as the other women listened. At the end of each reading, the four women used the CMW worksheet *(see Appendix 1)* to identify spoken and unspoken messages they heard in the respondent's reading.

Each woman then shared her comments on the reader's memory. All four women rewrote their responses incorporating group input from the first reading. The women repeated the CMW process using a second worksheet to capture reflections on the revised readings.

After a second round of sharing reflections, the women discussed the commonalities among their shared stories. Three had mothers who'd been domestics; two grew up in rural areas; three had earned master's degrees.

Three of us confirmed Lindsey's (1970) assertion of discovering our race difference outside of our homes. Diane accompanied her mother to work and overhead her mother's employer and her guests judgmentally discussing the texture of Diane's hair. Bernice noticed the different way that mud looked on her skin, versus the skin of her White playmates. As the only Black girl in dance class, Bernadette noticed the differences between her and the otherwise all-White class of dance students: she had brown skin, was taller than the others were, and wasn't wearing the obvious uniform – a pink tutu. Ruth realizes that she doesn't recall ever being unaware that she is Black.

In the follow-up session, three of the four women were present. The discussion centered on themes that surfaced from our memories and our subsequent inquiries of each others' experiences. We acknowledged knowing we were Black in our families and community of familiars. We also understood that our skin color made us different in the context of the larger society; and based on encounters with White culture, this difference was not a good thing. This insight came because of verbal or emotional diminishment from White people, or becoming aware of our difference in the context of a situational encounter.

In terms of new awareness, we discussed a recurrent theme: none of the four had told our parents about the diminishing interactions, or our new understanding of being viewed differently outside of our families. When probed about why no one told, participants raised the issue of concern for parents; "What could they do to avenge me that wouldn't jeopardize their safety or their livelihood?" One woman questioned, "When do we take on the role of protecting our parents? Do we protect our father more than our mother?" Additional questions raised included, "When and how does socialization to the survival mechanism pass down through generations?" and

"What brings children to the point of having to be concerned about economic needs?"

Participants in the full study followed the CMW protocol for conducting the sessions in the full research study, as well. Unlike the pilot group, these participants chose to forego the rewrite of their memory agreeing with one participant's assertion that, "Rewriting the memories compromises my memory." This is the only variation we experienced implementing the CMW process for the study. The group met six times to conduct the actual study; two people missed one session each due to work and family requirements. One person missed the follow-up session due to a last minute schedule conflict.

Limitations of the Study

The pilot study and the research study both engaged a narrow selection of participants who shared similar class backgrounds with the primary researcher. Participants are members of the primary researcher's informal network of friends and acquaintances. While some participants did not grow up middle class, each would be considered middle class today because of their present career situation and/or marital status. Using this design minimized the possibility of including poorly educated or currently poor women in this study. The primary researcher considered one woman of a lower economic level to participate; however, she is a co-worker. The primary researcher is a manager in the organization and this could have been perceived as coercive.

Becoming a Black Woman

Where

The CMW sessions took place in the Literacy room at the Winter Park Public Library. It is an intimate room with a circular table in the middle, and typically has three to five chairs arranged around the table. It has a bookshelf built into one wall, a ceiling to desktop level window next to the bookshelf, and a counter just below the window. Sessions took place on Thursday evenings from 6-9 p.m. The primary researcher provided fruit and cheese, fresh nuts and bottled water for each session.

Who: Sistahs at the Table

The women who participated in the main research study ranged from age twenty-one to sixty-eight. Two are retired, one was a senior-year college student and two are working professionals. Without design, we were two raised in the Northeast, two raised in the Southeast, and one born in the Northeast and moved to the Southeast at age eight. All of us currently reside in Orlando, Florida. Each accepted the invitation to participate as a way of supporting the primary researcher ~ and to see what we would uncover about our becoming Black women.

Barbara

The first person to accept my invitation was Barbara, a first-generation Haitian American woman. She is fifty-seven and the eldest of four children born in Manhattan, New York to Haitian immigrant parents. Her father owned several rental properties; her mother was a homemaker. At sixteen years old, she knew she wanted to be an attorney like her favorite uncle, "Ton-Ton Pierre" who lived in Paris, France. She was always drawn to books or her brother's toy trucks; she never saw herself as primarily a homemaker. Barbara's natural hair is a mix of light and sandy brown, cropped in a short style that frames her caramel colored, oval face.

At our first meeting three years ago, Barbara pulled into the parking lot of a local eatery driving her shiny, navy blue, Mercedes Benz CLK. She was dressed casually and had an air of assertive confidence about her. We introduced ourselves, I described my research, and she talked about her experience as a professional Black female in the academy. Based on my description-in-process, she agreed to participate in the study. Barbara is an intellectual, a critical thinker and a prolific writer; prior to becoming an attorney and law professor, she worked as a clinical psychologist. She is also a divorced mother of two sons in their twenties and a fifteen-year-old daughter, whom she admits to raising differently than her sons.

Barbara is stylish and sophisticated in a subtle way ~ not showy. I notice she carries a medium sized red designer shoulder tote with matching key fob and wallet. These, along with the Mercedes might be topics of conversation for others; Barbara wears them like a comfortable jacket. During the course of the study, she was invited to Italy to meet a potential research collaborator. Through her eyes, we learn that there is significant representation of Black women in Italy, and that many are coupled with older Italian men, apparently with no negative reaction from the general culture. This information piques our curiosity.

Ebony

At twenty-one she is the youngest participant in the study. Ebony is a full time student at the University of Central Florida. She formerly worked part-time in the children's department of a municipal library. Born in New York, her family moved to Florida when she was eight years old. Her mother is a real estate agent and her father is an electrician; she has one younger brother.

Ebony's skin is the color of swiss chocolate; she wears her shoulder-length black hair either pinned up, in a ponytail or cascading down. She has dark sparkling eyes sometimes shielded behind silver toned, wire-framed eyeglasses. Her personality bubbles forth in her easy laugh, which masks her deep introspective nature. When Ebony speaks, it is because she has something significant to say or a question to pose. Ebony is an independent thinker who has already decided that, while having a husband and children would be wonderful, neither one is necessary to complete her.

A birthday lunch with her grandmother at six years old taught her the power of money, delivered with a dose of respect. Her new classmates in Florida introduce her to the word "nigger" in third grade. [I note that White children know the word "nigger" as early as eight or nine years old, and how to use it.] At eight years old, the children in her new neighborhood - all boys - quickly let her know she isn't, and never will be, allowed in their male clubhouse. Ebony describes her parents' union as a loveless marriage. She believes they stay together for her and her brother's sake, yet both clearly see what their parents have yet to verbalize. These lessons have produced a self-assured young Black woman ready to make her independent mark on the world.

Jerelyn

We attend the same church and, until last year, were both members of the same Sunday school class; she eagerly accepted my invitation to be in the study. Jerelyn is brown-skinned and has shoulder-length, dark hair with light brown highlights and spare strands of grey. She was born in River Rouge, Michigan just outside of Detroit; the family moved within the city limits when she was eleven. Her father was a stevedore on the docks and her mother worked for the Internal Revenue Service. Her step-dad worked for Ford automotive. She was the first grandchild and has a younger brother.

Jerelyn is a retired corporate banking professional. She is a lover of learning and shares that in school, she was often singled out as "one of those smart kids." When she discovered her parents didn't have money to pay for her college education, Jerelyn found a job, moved out on her own at age eighteen and worked to pay her own way through college. She has also completed some graduate work. Her mother chided her for being too independent and warned that it would take her longer to get married; she first weds in her mid-thirties.

Jerelyn describes herself as "sixty and sassy". She is very assertive and often is first to speak in the dialogue. She is always meticulously dressed, even casually and prides herself on always being a lady. She has alert, curious eyes and you can often see her mind at work. Jerelyn is sure she wouldn't have survived enslavement or life in the South, pre-civil rights; she's convinced she would have run away or been killed for having a smart mouth. I can picture Jerelyn being a second-in-command to Harriet Tubman as she guided her underground "train" to freedom.

Joyce

Joyce is a former member of the Board of Trustees for my non-profit employer. She was born and raised in Winter Park, growing up on the city's predominantly Black West Side. Joyce and her sister were raised by their single mother, who was a domestic, and her grandmother, who took in laundry for the city's White residents. Her father worked in a New York department store as a custodian. She has a rich, dark brown skin tone and wears her hair closed-cropped, with salt-n-pepper strands framing her round face. Her dress is conservative, yet stylish and comfortable. She is graceful, possessing a warm essence that makes her easily approachable.

Joyce was Clerk for the City of Winter Park for twenty-three years and was the only Black Trustee on the board for six and a half years.

She takes pride in being able to get along with almost anyone believing that one does "attract more flies with honey than with vinegar." She is a divorced mother with two grown children – a son who works for the city and a daughter with sickle cell anemia for whom she cares. At 68 years old, she is the secretary for her church and can be found working there most weekdays. Many current and former White city officials as well as most Black residents seek her out for insight, counsel and guidance regarding affairs of the city.

Like most retirees, Joyce says she is busier now than when she was employed. She wouldn't trade her upbringing, poor as it was. In spite of the lack of material things, Joyce is comforted knowing she and her sister had an abundance of love from her family and community. She realized she was (and is) "a colored girl" at a very young age. This realization compels her child's eye to notice the differences in the way colored people were (and are) treated.

Ruth

She is the convener of the study and a participant observer in the experience. Ruth has medium brown skin and wears her hair in natural locks that fall just below her shoulders. At fifty-one, she has earned a bachelor's degree and three masters degrees. Her professional background consists of careers in broadcasting, corporate training, consulting, higher education, and non-profit management. Ruth is the third of five children raised in Awendaw, South Carolina, a rural community twenty-five miles northeast of Charleston.

Her mother is a retired registered public health nurse; her father owned and operated a service station and auto repair business. Of the five siblings in this Black middle class family, Ruth is known as the curious one, the risk taker. Her early childhood is shaped by her school and church experiences. She attended a private, Black Catholic school in Charleston – twenty-five miles away from her home community. This left her disconnected to peers in her community, and only somewhat associated with her schoolmates.

There was very little social connection with either peer-group. Books are her escape and her refuge; they feed her curiosity and love for learning, and inspire her adventurous spirit. Ruth has no children by birth; only nieces, nephews and godchildren. She has seen and interacted with Black women at various phases and stages of life in U.S. society. These interactions have prompted this study.

When the group assembled to study this topic, we brought our individual, group and societal selves into the discussions. Every experience we ever encountered as Black girls and Black women walked in the room with us. In her biographical documentary film *Writing a Life*, Puerto Rican author Esmeralda Santiago says "I am everything people have ever called me." This sound bite resonates with me. I interpret this to mean that every disrespectful, hurtful, insulting remark or action still lives with me. It also means that every uplifting, encouraging, praiseworthy comment or deed inhabits me, as well.

This research is contextually focused on race, gender and class. During the course of the study, we talked about nearly every facet of being Black and female. We recalled first memories of realizing we are Black and being treated differently because we are female. We reconnect to our first experiences of recognizing class difference, even though we didn't understand it until we were older. Reflecting on a particularly energetic round of discourse Joyce declares, "That's what makes it good to me. It took all that to get us from being Black girls to [becoming] Black women."

How: Elements of External Socialization

Earlier I mentioned the "triumvirate of senses" that forms Black girls' identity: senses of belonging, of identity and of control. The sense of belonging provides relationship and connection. The sense of identity helps her to define herself for herself; and the sense of control develops her resistance and resilience. I see this "triumvirate" as the keystone for Black girls' identity formation in US culture. These senses evolve early in her life and prepare her to navigate the world beyond her culture of familiars.

I propose there are three aspects of external socialization that Black girls plot a course through, to become Black women in the United States: 1) institutionalized oppression, 2) internalized oppression, and 3) resistance and resilience. Each is related to specific training fostered in early learning that stays with us into adulthood. Forms of oppression instill and reinforce subjugation in the contexts of race, gender and class. Resistance and resilience are taught as a means of survival by parents and others in the village[9] culture. While resistance and resilience each offer what appears to be some respite, I suggest that the mantle of oppression keeps Black girls and women in the United States operating in the continual mode of survivor.

Institutionalized and internalized oppression infuse what I consider negative indoctrination into Black girls.

> *"The person accepts society's view of her or himself as the "way she or he is", "the way things are." Negative judgments about that person become internalized and result in a self-image which reflects these negative ideas and beliefs. This usually becomes the expectation, and a self-fulfilling prophecy, which acts as a hindrance on development of the intellect and spirit. The person comes to dislike not only her or himself, but also her or his own people. For instance, women internalize society's negative attitudes about women and therefore have negative feelings and beliefs about themselves and all other women"*
>
> *(Tom Cummins et al., 1996, pp. section two - 6).*

Scott (1991) considers this negative indoctrination in her discussion of acculturated habits of survival – "they harden into ingrained attitudes – routines of thought, feeling, and action – that over time become unexamined and unquestioned traditions" (p. 8).

9 The "village" is a term from African culture, and still used in contemporary society. The nuclear and extended families comprise the child's "village"; these include core family, grandparents, aunts, uncles, neighbors, and the church, (i.e., "it takes a village to raise a child").

I believe our collective memory process reveals that this conditioning comes from the larger society, and may instinctively come from family because of their own upbringing and socialization. Our school and faith communities reinforce this training through peer and teacher experiences and via traditions that convey communal "wisdom." As we venture beyond our cultural familiars into the larger society media, the workplace, the legal system and government continue the indoctrination.

I maintain that resistance and resilience represent our sense of control and are positive aspects of Black women's preparation, as Barbara exhibits:

> *"If the premise is that you're only complete if you have this man, then we ain't going nowhere; we're right back where we started. We're still at that point, where some women will say, "I don't want to be treated like my grandmother was treated. I don't want to be dependent on 'if he doesn't give me $50 this week to go food shopping' ... I don't want to ever live like that. If it means that's what I have to not have, so be it."*

As stated earlier, these teachings typically come from the nuclear and extended family that may include the mother, grandmothers, aunts, sisters, or other "aunties" from the community (the village) and are quite intentional. A Black woman hears stories of ancestors who resisted and persevered, or witnesses the daily survival of women in her core family. I use the phrase, "may help" because not all Black girls are fortunate to have this early guidance, or are successful at exercising a sense of control in the face of oppression. Those who are able to hold onto a place of opposition, also often hold onto the stress of resisting and put their own personal health and wellbeing at risk (Neal-Barnett, 2003, p. 26).

I agree that socialization is inextricably linked with identity development for Black girls born and raised in the United States. "It is crucial to emphasize that race, class, and gender, are not fixed and discrete categories, and that such "regions" are by no means autonomous. They overlap, intersect and fuse with each other in countless ways" (Omi & Winant, 1994, p. 68). However, I contend that "knowing place" is defined and reinforced daily at the societal level as Barbara demonstrates in her reflection on Jerelyn's visit to the beauty shop.

> *"[She mentioned] the majority of the women in the shop had the same hairstyle, regardless of the length. The hairstyle is not the central issue; the beauty shop is a gathering place, it is not a place for individualization. It's a place where you go to become part of what's expected."*

"Keeping place" is taught at the individual level, and deemed justifiable at the group level. A Black girl learns this lesson as part of her socialization into the larger society, and it guides her maturation into womanhood.

Oppression

> *"Misinformation is the foundation of oppression. It has meant that various times during our history, U.S. citizens who considered themselves white have operated from the misinformation that people of color are inferior to them. This misinformation has turned into public and private, collective and individual laws, policies, attitudes, and behaviors that have excluded, discriminated against, injured, and killed people considered nonwhite."*
>
> *(Holtzman, 2000, pp. 159-160)*

Oppression is defined as "unjust or cruel exercise of authority or power; something that oppresses, especially in an unjust or excessive exercise of power; the act of subjugating by cruelty"(Parker, 2007). The capture and transport of our ancestors in the bellies of slave ships, over two hundred fifty years of legalized enslavement and nearly one hundred fifty years of legally sanctioned oppression bear witness to the historical subjugation of Black people in the United States. When I reviewed study participants' comments, the theme of "oppression" continually emerged from the data as we connected our life experience to our day-to-day encounters at the individual, group and societal levels. "Knowing place" underlies the theme of institutionalized oppression; "keeping place" occurs through repeated instances of internalized oppression. The laws and tenets of our society hold both processes firmly in place.

Institutionalized oppression is "institutional" because it is facilitated through recognized institutions in our culture, and reinforced from cradle to grave (Althusser, 1971; Omi & Winant, 1994). Racism is a form of oppression, as is sexism, and classism. When these differing "isms" are perpetuated by a social group against themselves, it constitutes distress patterns that Lipsky (1987) calls "internalized" oppression. These distress patterns "created by oppression and racism from the outside are played out by Black people upon members of our own social group and upon ourselves" (1987, p. 3). Institutionalized and internalized oppression are systemically linked to maintain the status quo of dominance and subordinance through institutions in our culture and through everyday behavior. I will discuss each separately in this section.

Institutionalized Oppression: The Politics of Knowing Place

> *"Whites were considered the superior race; white skin was the norm while other skin colors were exotic mutations which had to be explained. Race was equated with distinct hereditary characteristics. Differences in intelligence, temperament, and sexuality (among other traits) were deemed to be racial in character."*
>
> *(Omi & Winant, 1994, p. 15)*

As Barbara's summary of the beauty shop illustrates, we learn the politics of "knowing place" through multiple institutions in our society. These include the family, faith community, education system, government, the legal system, media and the workforce. Each body does its job to inculcate and/or emphasize what is considered acceptable behavior for social groups in United States culture. Louis Althusser (1971) referred to these institutions as *ideological state apparatuses* (ISAs). He considered societal institutions the conduits for implementing and sustaining systemic oppression throughout the culture.

These apparatuses endlessly reinforce the roles and societal beliefs of oppression as Barbara illustrates in this memory:

> *"When I practiced law in Philadelphia, I remember going with clients to the Union Club. The women had to go to the back door [to enter] and men could go in the front door. This was 1980 and these were women lawyers, women doing business. There are still certain clubs like that where women are only allowed during certain times."*

I contend that ISAs sustain the politics of knowing place that infuse the Black girl's socialization by repeatedly conveying to her hegemonic ideals of the dominant society. She may go on believing she should be treated differently because every institution she encounters says so. If she deviates from the blueprint, she receives negative feedback from other individuals and groups who follow the ideology consciously, or by rote performance.

Hegemony and Ideological State Apparatus

> *"It's always amazing to me how slavery is turned on its head as though slaves really are the ones who had the problems and not the people who enslaved them."*
>
> *Barbara*

Omi & Winant (1994) refer to Antonio Gramsci's notion of hegemony as "a popular system of ideas and practices" (p. 67) put forth by the dominant group. These ideas are made known and maintained "through education, the media, religion, folk wisdom" (p. 67) - Althusser's (1971) aforementioned ISAs - and accepted by the culture as "common sense." By producing and adhering to this line of "common sense" ideology, society gives consent to how it will be ruled (p. 67). Hegemonic rule legitimized "white" as good, right, and pure; and legalized "black" as bad, wrong and evil. Beverly Greene (1994), in her chapter on African American Women, states

> *"The dominant culture in the US idealizes the physical characteristics of White women and measures women of color against this arbitrary standard (Mays, 1985; Neal & Wilson, 1989). When compared to the White female ideal as the norm, traditional African features, darker skin, eye, and hair colors, broad or thick facial features, and kinky hair textures are deemed unattractive and inferior by the dominant culture*
>
> *(Collins, 1990; Neal & Wilson, 1989; Okazawa-Rey et al., 1987)" (1994, p. 18).*

This lesson begins early in a Black girl's life; it is reinforced through institutions and the individuals who maintain them.

My sister shared that several weeks ago, while combing her daughter's hair, my five-year-old niece, Tyler Lee told her she thought she had an itch. My sister, thinking she was reacting to an insect bite, told her to get the skin cream. Tyler Lee then indicated she just needed to scratch the brown off so her white skin could show. I am shocked and saddened that in 2007 my five-year-old niece believes that she needs to get rid of her pretty, brown skin. Tyler Lee's classmates are all Black or Latina/o children; she lives in a multicultural neighborhood of military families and her television viewing is limited to Dora the Explorer, Sponge Bob Squarepants, and the occasional movie. My sister and I are puzzled about where this idea came from.

Nearly sixty years ago, psychologists Kenneth and Mamie Clark discovered Black children learn to believe there is something wrong with the color of their skin at an early age. The Clarks conducted racial preference tests with Black preschool children from 1939-1950 using drawings and, black and white dolls. "Their early research established that societal rejection often resulted in a negative self-image in very young African-American children" (Abramovitz, 1997, p. 1568). The Clark's findings indicated that by age five, Black children are aware of the inferior status assigned to their social group based on the color of their skin. The study also showed that Black children accept this status through the recursive habits, beliefs and attitudes inherent in their social institutions.

The subtleties of our environments also deliver hegemonic ideas of the dominant culture. Joshua (2002) asserts that very young children "read" environmental print. They comprehend elements of the world around them without being able to decode individual letters or sounds (p. 125). Rogoff's (1990) *appropriation* theory in Goldberg, (2000) explains that children "adapt to traditions and agreements that constitute the institutions, norms, and technologies of their community" (2000, p. 347). Consequently, a student will imitate the internalized behavior of a teacher, a trusted/admired peer, or a significant adult in her/his life, upholding Rogoff's appropriation theory.

I posit that Tyler Lee absorbed the message of inferiority through the environment and routine activities of her five-year-old world. Whatever reinforcement she picked up was subtle; whether from media, interactions at school or in the family, or around her neighborhood. Clearly, hegemonic ideas permeate the minds of young Black girls on a daily basis. Spencer (1990) asserts that "young children are aware of the societal message that white is desirable. Fortunately, their perception that white is more desirable *does not* translate into a poor self image" (1990, p. 268) as concluded earlier by Shorter-Gooden and Washington (1996). It is also fortunate that the Clarks' study indicate this preference for whiteness decreases as children age.

According to Omi & Winant (1994) White Americans used "ethnicity theory" (p. 20) as an operating paradigm in early U.S. history, and assumed African Americans, Latina/os and Asian Americans would take on the ethnic roles defined by early European immigrants. Instead, each group resisted blindly assimilating into the melting pot and embraced *their* racial and cultural identities. The dominant culture overlooked the different geographical points of entry for these cultures and the societal context that initiated each group's move to this country. Omi & Winant point out two primary flaws with two ethnicity paradigms: *Bootstraps model* and *they all look alike*.

"The Bootstraps model" requires non Anglo-Saxon, non-White ethnic groups to modify and accommodate to societal "norms" defined by the dominant culture. The ethnicity paradigm assumes that because early Europeans assimilated, all other ethnic, that is racial, groups are also malleable and will assimilate. The model blames the group when it fails to incorporate "norms" defined by the dominant group. In other words, a Black child's failure to perform in a poorly equipped school is seen as the fault of the child, not a letdown by the educational system. The system assumes an "inherent deficiency" in the group and brings about failure because earlier white-skinned ethnicities [Irish, Italian, Dutch, etc.][10] have successfully assimilated and been accepted by the majority [White Europeans][11] (1994, p. 21).

"They all look alike" racializes a group by virtue of obvious physical features without respecting internal group variegation. National origin, religion, language, or cultural differences of Whites who comprised the European migration are not taken into account. Therefore, Haitians, Jamaicans, Afro-Canadians, native Africans and Guyanese are all seen as "black" by the dominant culture (1994, p. 22). "The paradigm is also applied to Native Americans, Latin Americans and Asian Americans"(p. 22). Omi and Winant define racial formation as the "sociohistorical process by which racial categories are created, inhabited, transformed and destroyed" (p. 55). Spencer (1990) sees

10 Brackets mine
11 Ibid

racial formation as the synthesized outcomes of societal interactions humans have with each other, what the dominant culture may prefer to call "the melting pot."

It appears to me that this model simplifies the melting pot notion for Whites; there's no need to be specific when "they" are all the same color. Everything is more comfortable for the dominant culture when "they all look alike". These interactions transpire daily as we all engage each other through social institutions. ISAs support and sustain institutionalized oppression on both large (government, the legal system, media, the workforce) and small (family, church, school) institutional scales. We facilitate our individual social construction while moving and living through these institutions.

I offer that hegemonic ideals are well engrained in young Black girls by the time the process of their socialization takes them beyond the home. Jerelyn and Barbara discuss this delineation specific to gender roles and household chores:

> *"Certain things were just boys' jobs versus girls' jobs." (Jerelyn). "She says 'there were her brother's jobs which were different from her and her sisters' jobs' so there's gender identification in what are boy's jobs and what are girl's jobs. There seemed to be a very distinct understanding of the two." (Barbara).*

The diminishment of young Black children - girls in particular - in US society has continued well past the early 1950's when the Clarks carried out their initial test. I recall a late 1980's news special where then-ABC News anchor Carol Simpson repeated the Clarks' doll test with elementary public school children. Teen filmmaker and documentary producer Kiri Davis repeated the same test with elementary school students in 2006. Both replications netted the same results: Black children saw the white dolls as prettier, as good and the black doll as bad and ugly, even though the black doll looked like them.

I propose that the education system fails Black children in general and Black girls in particular, when it omits the significant contributions that Black people have made to US history. In an interview on NBC TV's Today Show in the late 1980's, then Secretary of Education, William Bennett was asked if he thought there was any benefit to revising the history curriculum of US schools to accurately reflect all the contributions made by people of color. He responded, "I see no relevance for students to learn any history outside that of Western society ... there is no benefit in revising our history curriculum."[12] Consequently, Black students are forced to check their culture at the schoolhouse door and become a non-person, while continually resisting hegemonic notions of who society thinks they should be.

Instances like this are what I believe to be beyond the Black girls' sense of control. I liken this behavior to what Woodson (1933) calls the psychosis of being a good American and a good Negro.

Giddens (1984) defines structuration itself as "the conditions governing the continuity or transformation of structures, and therefore the reproduction of social systems" (p. 25). His structuration theory accounts for the reproduction of social life as well as its skillful production (Livesay, 1989, p. 265). In other words, systems utilize rules and resources to initiate social practices, experienced as "habits," that dictate how society operates and how humans behave in that society. Social institutions in the United States were established upon the "common sense" notion of oppression. Through institutions and through "habits," the powerful oppress the powerless; and in so doing, constrain the powerless to agree with their oppression. The discussion that follows shows how the dailyness of oppression is reinforced through each one of Althusser's (1971) defined ideological state apparatuses (ISAs).

Church/Faith Community

> *"If a man may preach because the Savior died for him, why not the woman seeing he died for her also? Is he not a whole*

12 As seen by the author

> *savior, instead of a half one, as those who hold it wrong for a woman to preach would seem to make it appear?" Jarena Lee*
>
> *(Billingsley, 1999, pp. 135-136)*

Nearly every Black church I ever attended had a White Jesus in its sanctuary hanging on the cross, or in photographic illustrations throughout the building. The funeral-home calendars and hand-fans donated by mostly Black morticians all depict similar images: Christ gazing out from the picture, kneeling at the Mount of Olives, or a pair of white hands clasped together in prayer. In Revelations 1:14-15, the Bible describes Jesus as having "hair like wool ... feet unto fine brass, as if burned in a furnace" (Lawson, 1988, p. 884). Given the region of the world and the climate of the times, it would seem a Jesus with skin like burnt brass would be a more honest reflection. Yet, the image of the good and benevolent White Savior saturates Black consciousness every Sunday; however, I digress.

I was raised in a Black Baptist church in rural South Carolina. My mother is Baptist and my father is African Methodist Episcopal. My grandfather co-founded the church I was baptized in; my mother was the Sunday School Superintendent while I was growing up. My siblings and I were raised in my mother's church, and we attended an all-Black Catholic school in Charleston, South Carolina. This multi-faith upbringing developed a unique perspective for a Black woman raised in the rural south and broached unanswered questions for me.

Women were excluded from the pulpit in all aspects of my faith experience growing up. They were relegated to serve on the Missionary, Usher, or Deaconess Boards – female designated positions that render support to chosen leadership. At the annual Women's Day observance, a female was allowed to grace the pulpit, with some murmurings among pulpit associates and from the pews. In the Catholic tradition, priests administered the sacrifices and conducted Mass; I never saw a nun venture near the altar or step onto it. Women were consigned to secondary status in all these faith traditions; what

I saw women doing in the church didn't fully translate to what I read about many women in the Bible, like Esther, the Queen of Sheba or Priscilla. Jarena Lee's quote resonated for me before I learned of her or read her statement.

Pre-enslavement, women in African culture were revered in spiritual practice; they were priestesses, queens, midwives, diviners and herbalists (Mbiti in Lincoln & Mamiya, 1990, p. 276). Acculturation into colonial America stripped African women of these revered roles. What the dominant culture did to Blacks through racial oppression, Black men did to Black women in the church through gender oppression. Jerelyn asserts, "They took the natural order God created ... and "lord" it over women as this is what He intended." Religious ideology in the Black community was enforced through racism and sexism as newly freed Black men seized and held onto positions in church leadership (Edwards, 2006).

Jacquelyn Grant (1982) in Collins (2000) considers "the church as one key institution whose centrality to Black community development may have come at the expense of many of the African-American women who constitute the bulk of its membership" (2000, p. 87). According to Lincoln & Mamiya, the church is the one place in society where Black men see themselves in a position of power. As a result, Black women still struggle to be officially recognized preachers and pastors in traditional Black faith denominations. Grant asserts, "It is often said that women are the 'backbone' of the church. It has become apparent to me that most of the ministers who use the term are referring to location rather than function. What they really mean is that women are in the 'background' and should be kept there (1982, 141)" (2000, p. 87).

When the Founding Fathers set out to establish Anglo-American culture in the United States, their focus was on a "unified American culture" (Spring, 2004, p. 8). Whites who owned human property in the 1500-1600s used the church as a management device. During enslavement, Whites preached a message of strict obedience that they connected to the teachings of the Bible. Controlling enslaved

Africans, Native Americans and the influx of Irish immigrants was the motivation for this ploy (p. 8). Noah Webster believed the standardized American dictionary of the English language, a spelling book and an American version of the Bible helped to formulate [and achieve] this unified national culture (p. 8).

Social construction theory asserts that individuals are born into existing social structures that define the roles for individual conduct (Althusser, 1971; Butler, 1990). Althusser (1971) includes the church as an institution in his discussion of ideological state apparatuses; he considers the church an important foundation in society with the power to reinforce ascribed social group behaviors or discount behaviors deemed outside the prescribed norm. Giddens (1984) in Stacey (2001) submits that, "human subjects and social institutions are jointly constituted through recurrent practices. The properties of the individual mind and of social practices do not exist outside action but are constituted in it" (2001, p. 61).

Butler (1990) argues that we come into the world and step into the role already established for us. We are simply characters on a pre-set stage, acting out a predetermined role. This supports Stacey's deduction that "social structure always exists prior to any individual actor" (p. 49); and Giddens' (1984) notion of joint constitution (p. 61). According to the church, social roles and expected behaviors are prescribed for women, men, and children. Each is expected to follow their social group script. This delineation has and continues to reinforce the values and paradigms of male patriarchy and female subjugation in the Black church.

Education System

> *"Real education means to inspire people to live more abundantly, to learn to begin with life as they find it and make it better, but the instruction so far given Negroes ... has worked to the contrary."*
>
> *Carter G. Woodson (Woodson, 1933, p. 29)*

Race, gender and class inequality in our education system nurtures structured inequality in the United States. It is sustained through inaccurate or inadequate curricula and by instructors who pass on to their families and to their students the same prejudices they were taught (Edwards, 2005)Race, Class, Gender</keyword></keywords><dates><year>2005</year></dates><publisher>Fielding Graduate University </publisher><work-type>knowledge assessment</work-type><urls></urls></record></Cite></EndNote>. Ebony recalls her first encounter with what I call institutionalized racism at her new school. For the first time, she is in the minority as one of four Black students in her third-grade class. The entire group of students is summoned to the school nurse to be tested for lice. From her pre-typed clipboard, the nurse reads off Ebony's and the other Black students' names to separate them from the others; they are told that they will not be tested.

> *"After school that day, we all got on the bus to go home; some of my classmates rode my bus. They begin drowning me in their inquiries as to why I didn't have to get my head checked. I told them I had no idea what lice were before today and didn't know why my name was called off the list. When the bus pulled up to my street, I went to get off and as I was walking alongside the bus to get to the house, a boy from my class spit on me and screamed 'you're a nigger; nigger's don't get lice' and started laughing."*

I perceive several aspects of institutionalized oppression at work in this scenario. First, the teacher and the nurse have obviously been taught that Black people didn't get lice and perpetuated the lie with this group of children. This is a fallacy: when I worked in upstate New York the summer of my sophomore year in college, we had to send back an entire camp – four busloads – of Black and White inner-city children because they were infected with lice. Second, as the adults in this situation, the teacher and nurse ignored the group dynamics brought on by their actions; if they did recognize the dynamics, they had no regard for the potential repercussions their behavior would heap upon the Black students. Third, someone had taught Ebony's young classmate the term "nigger" as another name for a Black person, and that it was okay to denigrate a Black person by spitting on her.

Woodson (1933) argued that every institution put in place to develop, support and sustain Black people's presence in the U.S. is oppressive. The family, the school, and the medical profession – each recognized as a foundational institution of our society – colluded in this scenario to diminish Ebony and her Black classmates. Joyce points out the irony of a good thing simultaneously being bad for these Black children:

> *"If this had been a Black school and the same thing was going [on] and someone said, "you know Black folks don't get lice" it would have been a different response because that's one less thing we gotta worry about. It's almost like taking something that's one less thing you have to worry about and making it a negative given the connotation that it was placed in."*

This incident brings to mind my earlier recollection of former Secretary of Education William Bennett's claim that the history curriculum used in US schools doesn't need to expand beyond Western society. I was astonished and disturbed by this comment then and still am now. School curricula were (and still are) used to perpetuate the hegemony of White intellectual superiority and the educational inferiority of Black people. Holtzman (2000) supports my assertion when she charges that U.S. schools provide limited and often distorted information about our country's racial history (2000, p. 205). She highlights the following:

- "Our textbooks present a glossed over version of history that excludes the brutal reality of the slave trade;
- [Black] families in both Africa and the United States suffered dissolution;
- Millions of Africans transported in the Middle Passage died before reaching their destination;

- Enslaved people were treated in a dehumanizing manner during the founding of our country" (2000, pp. 205-206).

As long as our educational system is used to convey an inaccurate version of United States history, the system of oppression will be supported and consistently reinforced through the institution of education as an ideological state apparatus.

The Legal System/Government

> *"I'm thinking from a historical standpoint, as well as biblical; where women are ... you're just a step above a slave. You can have my children, but I expect you to sit over there in that corner and be invisible. I don't expect anything from you because you're subservient."*
>
> *Jerelyn*

My research of ideological state apparati shows the legal system has been instrumental in maintaining the subjugation of women almost from the inception of our country. One's attention often turns to the police and the courts when thinking of our legal system. While they are the immediate purveyors, the system extends all the way up to the U.S. Supreme Court. Hine, Brown and Terborg-Penn (1994) assert, "the 'law' is the words in the Constitution, how the courts interpret those words, how enforcement authorities decide to enforce them and how the Constitution and the statutes and the governmental regulations as written, interpreted, and enforced operate together" (1994b, p. 701). The legal system is another institution that discriminates against Black women based on their race and on their gender. I find it interesting that Black women are seemingly included in the broad scope of the law regarding subjugation; however, have been excluded from consideration by the word of the law since the founding of the country.

Omi & Winant's (1994) theory of *racial formation* describes "American" identity as white. By this definition, Black women are negated in law and custom, public institutions, and forms of cultural representation through a broad scale hegemonic ideal.

> *"The legalization of race [is] underpinning everything; where everything is legalized by race. Understand, everything ... whether you go to the store, whether you get on the bus, whatever you're doing, or whether you go to church, where you live it's all dictated by a legalization of one's experience."*
>
> *Barbara*

The Black woman's dual target (race and gender) status as an oppressed group means we suffer equally with Black men and White women (Hine, Brown, & Terborg-Penn, 1994b, p. 702). Our reality is that we share a history of enslavement with Black men, yet we are economically valued and paid less than Whites and Black men because of our gender. "In the unlikely event Black men were to get any benefit under the law, Black women would not get it, for they were women" (p. 702). Research shows the same held true for our shared gender status with White women; any gender-ascribed benefit they would garner would exclude Black women because of their skin color.

According to Rowland (2004), when the US Constitution was ratified in 1791, descendants of enslaved Africans and women were excluded from the "we" in *We the People*. Both groups were considered less than fully human, therefore not entitled to equal protection or privileges under the law, as rendered to White men. Biology was the deciding factor that established their place in the social hierarchy as somewhere lower than men were (2004, pp. 18-19). During the study, participants discussed violence against women, battered women and the fact that many had no options for escape. Joyce offers,

> *"Some Black women [who stay in abusive relationships] believe they're acting in the best interest of the children. That's a concept that's been established in [her] mind that 'I need*

to stay there for the children's sake.' Some people do that because it's been instilled."

Barbara concurs: "And women used to do that because they had no alternative, no money. My mother [said to me] "I have four children, don't have an education like you have; I am totally dependent on your father."" I believe this speaks to the class subjugation of Black women as earlier defined by Lips (1999). Omi & Winant (1994) remind us that the United States has always been "an extremely "color conscious" society" from its inception. Race has defined political rights, geographic mobility, position in the labor market, and sense of identity. As such, racist action backed by law was equally meted out against Native Americans, Mexicans, Asians, and African Americans (1994, p. 1).

Historically, according to Hine, et al (1994), the legal system upheld enslavement, manipulated voting districts, and forced segregation in residential neighborhoods and schools for Black people. The American legal system is specifically unfavorable to those who are both *Black* and *women*. The law has denied women the right to vote, the right to own property, and dictated control of our reproductive systems, in the past and still today. When changes in some state laws protected women from having to farm or pay taxes, Black women were excluded from this privilege. Wage labor laws were no different; the government recommended to employers who hired former slaves that payment to Black men be $10-12 per month while Black women were to be paid $8 per month (1994b, p. 702).

Hine, et al cites three laws in the state of Virginia prior to the Civil War that legally sustained Black women's oppression:

> *"The first law provided that it was not unlawful for a white man to have sex with a Black female slave; the second stated that it was unlawful for whites to marry Blacks, whether those Blacks were slave or free; and the third law stated that the decision as to whether a newborn infant would be slave or free would depend on the legal status of the mother. If the*

> *mother was a slave, then the child would be a slave; if the mother was free, the child would be free"* (1994b, p. 702).

The state of Virginia held that a Black woman had no ownership of her own body. She had no way to legalize consensual sexual interactions, and no way to legitimatize her children in the eyes of the law.

As recently as 1967, over 100 years after the end of the Civil War, the miscegenation law was still on the books in Virginia. Loving vs. Virginia is the case of an appeal filed in the US Supreme Court by Richard Loving and his Black wife, Mildred Jeter. The two married in the District of Columbia in effect, circumventing their home state's ban on interracial marriage. They were charged and sentenced to one year in jail. The trial judge suspended the sentence for a period of twenty-five years on condition that the Lovings leave the state and not return *together* for 25 years (Cohen & Hirschkop, 1967).[13]

In Missouri, a law ascribed to protect "any woman" was dismissed in the case of an enslaved woman named Celia who killed her White master for repeatedly raping her; the judge ruled that she was not included in the phrase "any woman". An 1859 Mississippi law held that enslaved women had no rights to their body, and could not be violated by rape (Hine, Brown, & Terborg-Penn, 1994b, p. 703).

In her course summary for "Gender and the Law," University of Dayton Law School Professor Vernellia Randall proposes four rationales and ideologies that provide a historical context for women's legal position within United States society:

1) Legal subordination assumes that men represent a normal fully human being while women represent a usually inferior deviation of this entity.
2) Enslavement legalized the societal concept of women as property and perpetrated their direct exploitation for economic profit.

13 This case was argued April 10, 1967 and Decided June 12, 1967. The Supreme Court overturned the state ruling as a statutory scheme to prevent marriages between persons solely because of racial classification.

3) In post-abolition America, all women were steered into low-paying personal service jobs that curtailed prospects for earning a livable wage and reduced opportunities for training; for many Black women this is still the situation.
4) Legalized sexual exploitation of enslaved Black women, the nineteenth century "cult of motherhood," officially authorized

bans on birth control and abortion; domestic violence and laws against miscegenation contributed to define sexual norms that established and reinforced gender subordination; these often intersected with race and class subordination" (Randall, 2004, pp. 1-2).

Media

> *"Nevertheless, a 1998 survey revealed that only ... four out of ten African American children say they see people of their race "very often" on TV, compared to seven out of ten white children. The impact of this lack of images of people of color is significant for everyone in that it signals who is important in US Society."*
>
> *(Holtzman, 2000, p. 253)*

Along with receiving biased history in the classroom, mass media spreads the hegemonic ideal of what and who is acceptable in US society. Media has never been affirming of Black people in the United States – at least not consistently during my lifetime. My childhood memories are of the "Amos n' Andy" parody on television; the talented Bill "Bojangles" Robinson playing the happy butler/valet/waiter in a secondary role to 6 year-old Shirley Temple; "Stimey" and "Buckwheat" on Our Gang; and "Steppin'" Fetchit portraying the slow-witted, lazy, janitor/cabin boy/shoeshine man/whatever in countless movies. Of this collection, "Sapphire" of the "Amos n' Andy" program was the only Black woman featured in the media; and her role presented Black women as emasculating.

White (1999), states that during enslavement hegemony ascribed Black women to one of two roles: "Jezebel" or "Mammy." Myths about Black women became part of the slave lexicon and subsequently part of US culture reinforced through its institutions. Plantation owners created the conditions to populate their workforce and accused Black women of being lascivious when they had no control over their bodies and how they were used (1999, pp. 29-31). Journalist and author Lena Williams (2000) writes, "stereotypes may begin at home, but they are often spread through the mass media, white-owned institutions that help shape our opinions, views, and understanding of each other" (p. 162). When I was in college, we used to joke that any Black actor who played a role in a movie would be dead in the first ten minutes. If the actor was a woman, I could count on her portraying a whore, an emasculating "Sapphire" character, or a "welfare queen."

Today, the pervasive image of Black girls and young women portrayed in entertainment media as the "whore" or "hoochie" (Collins, 2000, p. 83) supports the hegemonic script by emphasizing the "jezebel" archetype.[14] Collins counts schools, news media and government agencies as important sites for transmitting "controlling images" that support the prevailing negative imagery of Black women and spreading those images across the globe (2000, p. 85). As the mother of an adolescent Black girl, Barbara thinks it's important to monitor all facets of society that feed into young people's acculturation.

> *"I look at those videos because I want to know what they're doing. VH1 and BET are just disgusting; they need to shut that one down. You sit there and you look at these young women and you might as well have sex and be done with it, because you don't have any clothes on anyway; you might as well just keep going."*

14 A full discussion of the tern "archetype" is presented under the next element of external socialization – Internalized Oppression – in the sub-section titled, "scripting."

According to NCCJ, we learn stereotypes about others, specifically from "our parents, friends, teachers and what we see on television, in movies, and what we read" (Birdsong et al., 1995, p. 40). When I facilitated an exercise entitled *"Things I Learned Growing Up ..."* (p. 40), participants often remarked that they learned mostly negative and stereotypical information about different social groups. I believe it's important to point out that the exercise offered two areas as the sources of the information: "family, teachers and friends" or "TV, books and magazines." Each of these areas include institutions Althusser (1971) identifies as ISAs. We all receive the same learnings from the same sources about ourselves and about "the other."

A recent survey of minorities and women in television and radio by Papper (2005) showed that while the minority population is 33.2% in the United States, only 21.2% of minorities work in television and 7.9% comprise the radio workforce. Further, regarding employment positions in broadcast media, women are most likely to be "news assistants, producers, reporters, anchors, writers, executive producers and assignment editors (in that order)" (Papper, 2005, p. 32). The report cites women as being the majority in three positions that have the least amount of power regarding what actually makes it to broadcast: news assistants, producers and reporters. The persons making this crucial decision in newsrooms are predominantly White men. With this advantage, the dominant culture is able to continue putting forward hegemonic notions for public consumption that support the ideological state apparatus.

As I write this, the country is immersed in a controversy over a syndicated White radio talk show host's racist and sexist remarks about members of a Black female college basketball team. The disparaging and diminishing phrase he used was "nappy-headed 'hos." The term "nappy" holds no weight by itself; "nappy-headed" alludes to unkempt hair that falls short of Americanized standards of beauty – a "target" position (Hardiman & Jackson, 1997) Black women find themselves in often. Combined with the diminishing term "'ho" – a derivative of the word "whore" – the phrase stirs up images of the "promiscuous Jezebel" (Stephens & Phillips, 2005, p.

39) archetype ascribed to Black women. The announcer feels that frequent use of the terms by those in the music industry – particularly by Black male rap and hip-hop artists – in reference to Black women gave him the right to say those words too.

When I first read the story in *Diversity Inc.*'s online newsletter, I experienced a visceral reaction. Other Black women across the country that I spoke with said they *felt* the comments as well. It was as if we connected to the sting of those words and they echoed through a "collective conscious." I offer that this "collective conscious" is what Wilson (1978) calls "group conscious." According to Wilson, "the person then identifies [her]self and the group as one and the same, and thus any unfair attack against the group is seen as an attack upon the person [her]self. Any degradation of the group is felt as a degradation of the self" (1978, p. 160). This confirms my intuition that many Black women and young girls "felt" those diminishing remarks by virtue of this collective consciousness.

Workforce

> *"From the intricate web of mythology which surrounds the black woman, a fundamental image emerges. It is of a woman of inordinate strength, with an ability for tolerating an unusual amount of misery and heavy, distasteful work."*
>
> *(White, 1999, p. 27)*

Collins (2000) states that West African women were used to combining "work" with family duties. Childcare involved bringing children to the fields, introducing them to the family business of selling products at the market, and tending and harvesting crops. At the appropriate age, children assumed responsibilities that supported the family, i.e. caring for siblings, running errands and in general, lending a hand. "Working did not detract from West African women's mothering; being economically productive and contributing to the family-based financial system was an integral part of motherhood" (2000, p. 49). Collins reminds us that the separation of public work as paid employment from unpaid private work in the home was never a reality for Black women.

Historically, most Black women worked outside the home; there was never a choice to do otherwise. I posit that enslavement forced a paradigmatic shift in Black women's roles at home and at work. During enslavement, the Black woman was not paid for her public work since her designated status as inhuman negated consideration of her as an employee; all profits belonged to the plantation owner. She and her family belonged to the owner as well, and were subject to auction at any time, so there was no private sphere of work, i.e. home to maintain. As progenitor and caretaker of the plantation's workforce she was, in essence, the first human resources manager in our agrarian society.

I believe White's (1999) opening quote to this discussion of the workforce brings up a notable aspect of this dynamic. Enslaved African women were not given a choice about what types of work they would do in colonial North America, nor the option to be "stay at home" moms. Hegemony facilitated the oppression of Black women in the workforce; she engaged in manual labor just as the Black man did.

> *"If one assumes that real men work and real women take care of families, then African-Americans suffer from deficient ideas concerning gender. Black women become less "feminine," because they work outside the home, work for pay and thus compete with men, and their work takes them away from their children"*
>
> *(Collins, 2000, p. 47).*

Gender role separations for Black people were muddled when compared to Whites. Black women worked in the fields alongside Black men during the practice of slavery. Today, Black women continue to work outside the home. In the pilot study, three of the four women's mother worked as a domestic and one's mother was a nursing professional. Three of the five women in the full study had mother's who worked outside the home; Joyce's mother took in laundry for White residents and Barbara's mother was a full-time stay-at-home mom.

Following enslavement, Black women continued to work in the fields or worked as domestics to supplement family income. As far back as I remember all the women in my nuclear and extended families worked outside the home. There was never an option for them to be Stay-at-Home Moms. Four of us in the research study group come from working mothers and grandmothers who were employed outside the home, co-managed a family enterprise, or ran some type of income generating business while taking care of home and family.

> *"My first grandmother that died took in people and helped them out. I guess he would have been homeless if she hadn't helped him, and he ran errands for her. People that had bigger houses could rent them out; if they were widows, they [would] rent out back rooms that were unused. My other grandmother had five bedrooms and she rented out the three back rooms to single men. That way you would have men in the house and that was additional protection."*
>
> *Jerelyn*

In the "Bronx slave market" Black women stood in assigned spots on the street and waited for employers to drive by and offer them day work (Collins, 2000, p. 56). According to Collins, it was not atypical for a White man to pick up a woman under the pretext of hiring her for housework, only for her to arrive at the house and realize the man wanted to have an affair (2000, p. 56). This lends a different frame of reference to the term "streetwalker" as we know it today. I believe this practice was somehow transferred to Black women, and linked them with the "Jezebel" archetype.

Giddings (2001) maintains that when the women's movement launched its efforts to help middle-class White women find work the initiative didn't resonate with Black women. White women wanted domestic freedom yet didn't want to do the low-skill, low-paid jobs relegated to women – the kind of work Black women performed (2001, p. 299). Giddings points to the ironic state of freedom middle class White women gained from domesticity that oftentimes came because Black women were running their households and caring for their children. This provided the avenue to career pursuit beyond the bounds of motherhood.

Collins posits that legally recognized racial and sexual discrimination relegated Black women to the bottom of the occupational hierarchy, to agricultural and domestic service and to unskilled service sectors. According to Collins, this group of alienated laborers can be economically exploited, subject to physically demanding work and intellectually deadening tasks. She defines alienated labor as paid – domestics, dishwashers, drycleaners, health care assistants, and professionals performing "corporate mammy work" – or unpaid, i.e., the continued childrearing of Black grandmothers and single mothers. Collins upholds the notion that Black women are the "mules" of our society (2000, p. 48) through her definition of Black women's historical association with this occupational area.

I acknowledge that other US institutions facilitate the oppression of Black women. However, I focused primarily on those institutions defined by Althusser as ideological state apparatuses (ISAs) for the purposes of this discussion. These ISAs have the best mechanisms for inculcating society's members into the recursive habits that Giddens (1984) speculates reproduces our established social systems. Oppression through the ISAs of family and church is reflected in the study participant's memories. Government-sanctioned institutionalized oppression is primarily entrenched in the legal and education systems, thereby threaded throughout our social structure. NCCJ offers that oppression through these ISAs may best be distinguished by considering the group that has established and sustained a system of power in the United States for 400+ years. I submit that group would comprise of White males, i.e. the "Founding Fathers" and their descendants.

Microaggressions: the Dailyness of Oppression

> *"The things you experience every day that then add up and take their toll. Everything from being in a place and feeling invisible or ignored or questioned about your credentials or your feelings about race matters. They may seem minor, but people don't know how much this society makes blacks constantly think about being black." Dr. Alvin Poussaint*
>
> *(Williams, 2000, p. 10)*

Black women are projected to be strong, emasculating, invulnerable and ultimately, unfeminine (hooks, 1981; Jones & Shorter-Gooden, 2003; White, 1999). During the study, participants engaged conversations on experiencing the 'lack of regard' society has for Black women in the US. We particularly discussed the ease with which people feel free to say anything to us, at anytime. Barbara recounts an upsetting moment on an elevator:

> *"I was teaching at Howard Law School and was pregnant with my second kid. I got on the elevator with a Black man who was a professor – who was obviously older than I was – and a bunch of students and he said to me "Oh I see you been fucking.""*

She recalls feeling embarrassed by the comment, that it was delivered by a professional colleague, and that it was witnessed by students.

Jerelyn shares that a bank administrator tells her, "You are the sexiest young thing" during her application process for a promotion. Ebony discloses an encounter in a club where "a guy grabs your booty and asks for your phone number. He accuses you of "being stank" (thinking you're better, being uppity) if you refuse his advances."

These are some examples of what I call the "dailyness of oppression" and what Barbara terms "spirit-murdering" that Black women deal with, day in and day out. Oftentimes we remain silent about these attacks; Joyce suggests that sometimes we say nothing [in the presence of these attacks]; "that's called surviving because that's the way we get through it."

White women may encounter similar behavior that for them is exclusively *sexist*. The experience for Black women is compounded by *racism* and *sexism*. Nearly forty years ago Chester Pierce (1970) coined the term "offensive mechanisms" to define "the small, continuous bombardments of micro-aggression by whites to blacks ... in race relations and race interactions" (p. 263). He said it was crucial that Black people learn how both *Blacks and Whites* project pro-racist attitudes that allow Whites to continue to dehumanize Blacks. Pierce believed that understanding micro-aggression would help Blacks learn to live better and longer (p. 282).

These little insults may be subtle or fully blatant; Joyce shares her experience of a circuitous act microaggression.

> *"I worked in the administrative office of the city for seven years. A new mayor was elected and he was from the old school, regarding his thoughts and beliefs about Black females. During the election, the office was somewhat involved. At the celebration, everyone in the office got invited – I didn't know there was a party; didn't think anything about it."*

Solorzano, Ceja, and Yosso (2000), in their study of collegiate racial climate and micro-aggression reveal that, despite Pierce's caution, nothing has yet been done to prepare African Americans to manage these "nicks" when they experience them (p. 2).

"Indeed, it is typically in subtle and covert ways (i.e., private conversations) that racism manifests itself. These innocuous forms of racist behavior constitute racial microaggressions" (2000, p. 2). Ruth recalls a direct encounter with microaggression that happened in a private conversation:

> *"I was having a conversation with one of my staff members about her behavior during a meeting and she says, 'Well, here you are, this big, Black, super-Amazon' and no one pays attention to me; I feel invisible.' The look on my face tells her she's crossed a line, so she counters with 'That's a good thing.' I tell her it's not because the tone in her voice wasn't affirming, and not to ever repeat that to another Black woman. It took me the next 24-hours to process that, with phone calls to Sistahfriends in Atlanta, California and DC, and a White ally in New Mexico."*

For Black women, incidents like those mentioned above are compounded in this society's racist and sexist hegemony. Greene (1990) asserts

> *"The pressure of racism and the varied effects and methods used by Black parents to minimize its damaging effects on their children can be accurately perceived as a major source of stress not shared by their white counterparts. It is reflected in the amount of energy consumed in, and the distractions presented by, the ongoing requirements of coping with the dominant culture's prejudices and barriers" (1990, p. 215).*

We need to be fully armored to survive the continuous onslaught of micro-aggressions that await us everyday. Bell & Nkomo (1998) define "armoring" as "an adaptive mechanism for coping with racial oppression" (p. 285). They maintain that before sending us out into society, our families hope they have embodied us with sufficient levels of respect, courage, self-reliance, and strength to sustain our wholeness (p. 285).

I think it's important to acknowledge Pierce's admonition of micro-aggressive tactics used by Blacks and Whites. Joyce recounts a situation in her workplace:

> *"Earlier when I was working for the City there were two "Joyces" in the same general area. We nicknamed each other "OJ" for the White Joyce and I was "BJ" meaning Black Joyce; she was "OJ" meaning other Joyce because I was there first. We shared that with each other and it was cordial; but then the outsiders started calling me "BJ" and it wasn't cordially ... they put another spin on it. So then I had to draw the line and say 'My name is Joyce and that's what you will refer to me as.' So that's how they take something that could be – you know, it was just a friendly thing with us; my co-worker's daughter started it so she could tell which one to ask for so it was a friendly thing with us. When it goes outside that realm that's when it becomes a problem; and that's when you have to know how to bring it to an end."*

During the study, each woman could recall another shared experience with microaggression. Each has had individual encounters with the "A" word – the frequent opportunities White folks take to tell Black people "you're so articulate." Cole (2006), in the article *"You're So Articulate"* cites the response a Black female executive said to her boss to help him realize this isn't a compliment.

> *"The reason it's not a compliment is because for the majority of people you deal with who are white, being articulate is a given. Somehow the point of reference is that if I am African American and articulate, it is by some miracle that I turned out that way"*
>
> *(2006, p. 56).*

This same articulation draws criticism from our Black community where the accusation is that you're "talking white." Ruth recalls hearing the term while growing up. "'Talking White' is a separation piece; it can separate you from your familiars; you're right there, but there is this ... 'she's not really like the rest of us' insinuation."

Jones & Shorter-Gooden (2003) point out the dissonance Black women encounter between balancing their accomplishments in the larger society with being perceived as someone who can still relate with their community of culture.

> *"In some circles of the Black community, Black women are expected to act "White" or "bourgie." Conversely, other segments of the Black community, in an effort to disavow anything resembling White folks, demand that she be "down home" or "ghetto." In addition, because the Black community is not immune to sexist norms, she may be pressed to be submissive and unassuming with her male partner at home" (2003, p. 83).*

This supports study participants' discussion of assimilative acts from Black culture. I maintain that in-culture assimilation is an aspect of internalization oppression, which I explore in the next section.

Internalized Oppression: The Politics of Keeping Place

> *"Patterns of internalized oppression get played out in dozens of unique ways in each individual. But we have come to recognize that there are certain forms of internalized oppression that are widely experienced by black people in our society."*
>
> *(Lipsky, 1987, p. 4)*

The five participants in this study all currently live in the Orlando, Florida area; as stated earlier, "knowing place" resonated for each of us in our memories of growing up. Joyce shares this memory of her first ride on a city bus with her mother and sister:

> *"She was a little colored girl who had to abide by the rules for colored folk. One great memory was the trip to Orlando*

> *to see the Christmas parade. They had to take the bus and this time there was standing room only so they stood and hung on to keep from falling. Once out of familiar surroundings, the reality that they were colored was very present. The way some folk looked at you made an unspoken statement: 'look at the colored children.' When she returned to the safe haven of West Winter Park, she knew she was definitely a colored girl and she began to notice the differences in the way colored people were treated."*

As you can see these memories are strongly connected to race and to gender, with undertones of class. Once you know your place, ISAs structure members of society to ensure you "keep your place." Joyce's home town of Winter Park, Florida was established in the 1800's. Whites lived in east Winter Park and Blacks lived on the West Side – they still do today. The town is divided physically, economically, and racially by railroad tracks.

The Black community knew [and still knows] its place – to supply labor to the White residents on the other side of the tracks. At the end of the workday, Blacks were expected to get back to their place, across the tracks; they still do today. Joyce evenly states in her gentle voice,

> *"Whites and coloreds were separate but treated with respect, each in their own places. In fact, the dominant culture was the Whites and they didn't want to treat you the same; they wanted to be sure that you were treated differently because of the color of your skin. And anytime anybody would stand forward to be more like them it was a threat, and that's when you got the negative treatment."*

I contend that Lipsky's (1987) internalization theory is also applicable to gender oppression; women too have been "forced to perpetuate and agree to our own oppression"(1987, p. 1). Barbara charges: "You really can't blame men for women being where they are; other women teach you to hold yourself back, not to step outside the box and be whoever you want to be." Jerelyn asserts, "Mothers want daughters to become wives and mothers [because] it's a life they chose." Barbara tells of a friend whose daughter is a pre-medical student; the mother has told the daughter "it's time for you to get on the doctor track, that is, find a husband who plans to be a doctor." The mechanism of oppression remains the same despite the social group category being different.

I consider Lipsky's (1987) theory operable for anyone who is living life at or below the middle class level of society, as defined earlier by Cushner et al (2003). The other women in the study agreed that class status could cause separations. Joyce recalls the importance of owning property in Winter Park: "In this area, if someone owned property, it gave them status; in the minds of others that was a symbol of status." A parent's class status and any associated prejudice could also be directed to the children.

Study participants also defined a correlation between class, access to benefits and privileges and skin tone, as Barbara and Jerelyn share:

> *"But the light skin is class; the light [skin] is valued as something because if you were light you could do certain things that other people couldn't, like passing. I have a cousin, my uncle married a German and his children are everything from looking like me to very fair and one of them has passed. She has her mother's name and she married this guy and she moved over, I mean she has cut off her family and got nothing to do with them. Another friend's aunt left the South for Chicago and totally cut her family off because she could pass. So I think there's a value to that; you might have been poor, but you had that color thing and as long as you had that that was a value."*
>
> *Barbara*

> *"In a way it [skin tone] translated to 'it's worth something'; there were benefits because if the White people – especially in the South – couldn't tell you were Black they treated you as equals, they treated you as White. My husband's grandparents were two light skin people who married each other; all their children married dark skin people. There was a section where they [light skin people] kept marrying other light skin people so their children stayed light and fair and fair and fair. Some of them well, you know..."*
>
> *Jerelyn*

> *Genovese (1976) discusses the historic presence of this issue in the Black community:*

> *"The slaves," recalled Annie Laurie Broidrick of Vicksburg, Mississippi, in accordance with the plantation legend, "were of two classes; the bright (colored) darky who was trained for house service, and the 'corn-field nigger'; the latter being usually the black, shiny darky who could sleep all day ... the dining-room servants or butlers were usually mulattoes, who were great dandies, having all the graces and mannerisms of their masters ..." (p. 327).*

He goes on to say that there existed in Charleston, [S.C.], New Orleans, [LA.], and some other cities a preference for light-skinned slaves to work in the house. Beyond this, the practice was far from general (p. 327). There is an assumption in Black culture that light skin Blacks were treated better than dark skin Blacks. Genovese notes "mulattoes came to be preferred for house work roughly to the extent that they had acquired certain cultural advantages that made them more presentable to upper-class white society" (p. 328). He says caste lines were also more prominent in Charleston and New Orleans, a holdover from Caribbean tradition.

According to Genovese, the legend of the house-slave elite grew up primarily in the cities. "Those who might have formed an elite status group on the plantations constituted only a small minority of the total number of house slaves" (p. 328). This appears to correlate skin tone and class access. During enslavement, mulattoes and other light skin Blacks had access to the plantation owner's home and family. By working in this environment, they also could be in proximity to finer clothing, more upscale household and other accoutrements of "the big house." Of course, this would only hold true in situations where the owner and his family were of a higher economic station in White society (Genovese, 1976).

Okazawa-Rey, Robinson and Ward (1987) concur with Genovese and point out "color-consciousness is rooted in the social, political, and economic conditions that existed during the centuries of slavery in the US" (1987, p. 92). Having dark or light skin tone converges with the notion of "good hair" as an issue of internalized oppression for Black women. "Good hair" is defined by Bonner (1991) as "hair that's naturally straight, loosely curled or waved; those of us with the springy African hair were banished to "bad hair" purgatory, doomed to spend eternity making it look "good"" (1991, pp. 1-2). Okazawa-Rey et al support this notion when they cite the predominant description used by authors in the late sixties to early seventies, in their works about Black women. "Beautiful black women had long, flowing hair cascading down their backs, clear, light eyes, and finely-cut, well-molded features" (1987, p. 89).

The authors indicate that the family is often where Black girls learn the values attributed to differences in skin color; these color-conscious attitudes are then reinforced in the large society (1987, p. 90). They point out that for women in the US, self-concept partially develops from observing and internalizing what others think about her and that Black females accept society's label of "attractive" or "unattractive" because of this acculturation. Here, Okazawa-Rey et al concur with Parham, White & Ajamu's (2000) notion that Black people learn to view themselves based on what they are told by society about who they are and what their place is in society. Okazawa-Rey et al posit that Black women facilitate internalized oppression by owning and affirming the division between lighter-skinned and dark-skinned women (1987, p. 93). They maintain that this separation buys into the American standard of beauty and keeps Black women in double jeopardy responding to the "desires and expectations of black men and to white cultural values and norms" (1987, p. 99).

The women in this study – Barbara the attorney, Jerelyn the retired banker, Ruth the management professional, Joyce the retired city clerk, and Ebony, the daughter of a realtor and an electrician –would be considered middle to upper-middle class, as defined by Cushner, McClelland and Safford (2003). All but Joyce grew up middle class, having access to goods and services that others did not, and having family who owned property. Joyce defines the power and privilege that come along with owning real estate:

> *"Nobody had anything, in fact, but oftentimes the people they worked for gave them property or gave them a home, something like that. So that gave them, in the minds of others, a symbol of status and when they owned several properties, even if it was vacant, they owned it. The fact that they owned it caused people to look at them a little differently."*

The study participants range in skin tone from honey brown to semi-sweet dark chocolate. While no one shared specific incidences of skin tone discrimination, the women acknowledge and agree it is a divisive tool of class demarcation.

Whether clothing, school, organizational membership, occupation, or skin tone; class distinction is another oppression that serves to cordon one group from the other. The notion of "passing" supports this separation, as does old English dress codes and school uniforms. The woman who felt she had to sever all ties with her family in order to have a life of privilege and access suffers this separation, as does her family. Socio-economic class is a mechanism of separation, as discussed by Garber (1997) and Cushner et al (2003). I maintain that class separation is about who has power and access to benefits and privileges, and who does not as Jerelyn shares in the recollection about traveling to school.

> *"Once you got past fifth grade you had to go to school on the other side of town which was over by the salt mines. In between Marathon Oil, Ford Motor Company and the salt mines, that is where our school was. Southwest Detroit was primarily Italian, Hungarians and Blacks. We lived three blocks up off this main road, we were bussed; the people who lived three blocks down had to walk. Our houses were brick, their [those who lived by the salt mines] houses were wood frame."*
>
> *Jerelyn*

Race and gender have long been acknowledged as the double oppression for Black women (Cade, 1970; Collins, 2000; Davis, 1981; Giddings, 1984; Green, 2003; B. A. Greene, 1990; hooks, 1981; Jones & Shorter-Gooden, 2003; Mama, 1995; Pyant, 1991; Rosenberg, 2002; Scott, 1991; Shorter-Gooden, 2004; Shorter-Gooden & Washington, 1996; St. Jean & Feagin, 1998; Thomas, 2004; White, 1999). Race and class have also been connected as dual oppressions (Collins, 2000; Cushner, McClelland, & Safford, 2003; Davis, 1981; Green, 2003; Kirk & Okazawa-Rey, 2001; Scott, 1991; White, 1999). Race, gender and class are uniquely joined as Black female oppressions (Bell & Nkomo, 1998; Collins, 2000; Davis, 1981; Giddings, 2001; Green, 2003; Henriques, 1995; hooks, 1981; Randall, 2004; Scott, 1991; Shorter-Gooden, 2004; Shorter-Gooden & Washington, 1996; Thomas, 2004; White, 1999). The three work independently and collude where Black women are concerned. Together they influence Black female existence in the United States.

Internalized oppression provides a container for race, gender and class subjugation, bringing Lipsky's (1987) theory to fruition. I posit there are three facets of internalized oppression: scripting, performance and assimilation. Barbara shares this memory of her cousin who followed the societal script, while being affirmed that she could break the script in her life:

> *"That Christmas her older cousin Anne Marie came to visit from Chicago. She was married to a doctor and always had a certain air about her. She spoke of "us" and "Charles's practice" and "Charles says this or that" ... it was always about Charles; and never did she ever say a word about herself. 'Why does Anne Marie speak only of Charles?' she asked Ton-Ton Pierre. Because he is her life, she thinks that's what women are supposed to aspire to; it's another way of life, but that doesn't have to be your life."*

These characteristics often unfold in the socialization experience for Black girls becoming women in the United States. Scripting is the manual that informs behavior, as dictated by the ideological state apparatus. Performance is their implementation of the script. Assimilation is the act of honing performance to the point of looking and acting as much as possible like the dominant culture. The irony is no matter how hard she tries, a Black girl will never actually mirror a White girl – her gender equivalent in the dominant group.

Scripting

> *"Both learning and meaning about sexuality are transmitted through cultural contexts that, for African American adolescent women, are embedded in a unique gender and racial experience" (Stephens & Phillips, 2005, p. 38).*

The women in both the pilot study and the full research study nearly all had mothers who worked outside the home. Three were domestics, three were professionals and one took in laundry for White customers. Greene (1994) states, "Unlike many of their White counterparts, African American women are not socialized to expect marriage to relieve them of the need for employment. Their financial contribution to the household is usually presumed necessary" (1994,

p. 13). Barbara's mother was the only one who did not work outside the home; she was what we today would term a Stay-at-Home Mom.

Likewise, each of us works outside the home. We are all high school graduates; seven of us are college graduates and four of us have advanced degrees. One of the messages we clearly understood from our parents was that we needed to be able to take care of ourselves. That meant get a good education and be employable. Again, Greene (1990) supports this statement: "Young Black females are socialized to expect that they will have to work to support themselves as well as their families, to think about the kind of work they will do, and to educate themselves to obtain appropriate skills" (1990, p. 213).

Clearly, as study participants discussed, one of the earlier scripts that informed our behavior spoke to education, employment and self-sufficiency.

> *"If you don't have your own money you gotta get it from someplace. This is what I tell my nieces. So the key is to put yourself in a position where you have a steady income stream. There is no guarantee that your parents are gonna die and leave you this cash flow, ASAP. It's not gonna happen like that. Number one, I'm the administrator; you ain't gettin' it. What are you going to do? You have to raise your daughters to be productive citizens so they become self-sufficient. You have to earn a living somehow, you have to do something that brings in a steady income flow. It's easier if you have an education."*
>
> *Jerelyn*

These are messages from socialization by our cultural familiars, particularly our mothers, grandmothers, etc. The working woman script seems conventional, standard even considering Black women's history in this society. It was what we saw respectable Black women do. It is what our predecessors expect of us as Black women. The dominant society has other ideas of how they expect Black women to be.

At five feet ten and a half inches, I have often been called a "big Black woman." I've been this height since the eighth grade. Following a training session, one man indicated on his evaluation that he expected me to be 'more forceful and aggressive in my delivery because I was so tall.' The comment was absurd considering that I was facilitating career training and counseling to recently downsized individuals. Why would I be aggressive and forceful with a population that is typically in a state of distress? I suspect he was expecting a corporate version of the "Sapphire" archetype.

An archetype is a prototype or model. Stephens & Phillips (2005), in their study of sexual scripting processes for African American girls, expand upon White's (1999) assertion regarding foundational images for Black women's sexuality. "The promiscuous Jezebel, asexual Mammy, breeding Welfare Mama, and emasculating Matriarch all reflected the social, political, and economic value American society placed on African American women" (2005, p. 39). The *Black Feminist Statement* of the Combahee River Collective (1977) lists "mammy, matriarch, Sapphire, whore, [and] bulldogged as pejorative stereotypes attributed to Black women" (1977, p. 2). I contend these pejorative, pre-existing scripts reside in society's collective conscious and set up false assumptions about Black women in US society, as Barbara and Ebony demonstrate:

> *Barbara: "I have a fifteen-year old daughter who will be in the next generation. It's scary how they [men] speak to them [Black girls]; it's okay, it's okay to be called a bitch."*

> *Ebony: "Women in my generation call each other that and it's okay; it's how you refer to someone that's your girlfriend, your 'homey,' and you know ... that's okay. That's why there are a lot of things I started doing when I was a freshman that I don't do anymore, like going to clubs. Certain [ones]*

> *I've gone to you get that kind of ignorant behavior where the men, they're all like 'why you acting stank?' when you don't accept the fact the he just grabbed your booty and asked for your number. "*

Collins (2000), hooks (1981, 1984), Jones & Shorter-Gooden (2003), Scott (1991), Stephens & Phillips (2005), White (1999), and Williams (2000), among others, mention four, hegemonic, foundational images defined for Black women in the US. These are the "Mammy," the "Jezebel," the "Sapphire" or emasculating "Matriarch," and the "Welfare Mama." I think this is a good point to offer definitions for each of these images. We'll begin with the "Mammy" image. Hine, et al (1994) credit the Mammy figure as a remnant of plantation legend who has weathered the centuries and remains a powerful icon.

> *Mammy – "the myth of the Mammy revolves around two basic principles. First, that a slave woman within the white household devoted her maternal instincts and skills to the white family who owned her and that she took pleasure and pride in this service. Second, that she gained status from this role and was revered within the Black community. The roots of this myth are planted deep in Old South nostalgia. It is true that many Black women were forced to devote their time and energies to the white family in the "Big House," but most were not slave women of advanced age who lorded over the white household. Rather, most slave women who tended children were young, interchangeable nurses. The maternal affection Black women were alleged to have lavished on their white charges was more likely the mask demanded by racist slaveowners. White southerners wished to believe that slaves preferred white children to their own, not merely as a strategy for currying favor but as a recognition of white superiority. White employers have demanded this deception from Black household help well into the modern era"*
>
> *(Hine, Brown, & Terborg-Penn, 1994a, p. 744).*

The image of Jezebel ascribed to Black women originated during enslavement. The name comes from the Bible character whose wanton behavior and evil ways enticed Ahab away from God.

> *"Evil, idolatrous, reckless, rebellious, ungodly, wicked, and abuser of power are just a few of the descriptions associated with Queen Jezebel, who was also a Baal prophet. Jezebel is remembered for her evil in the sight of the Lord – her Baal worship and her cruelty to others"*
>
> *(McCabe, 1988, pp. 278-212).*

Collins (2000) links the image to that created during enslavement:

> *Jezebel – "The jezebel, whore or "hoochie" is central in this nexus of controlling images of Black womanhood. Because efforts to control Black women's sexuality lie at the heart of Black women's oppression, historical jezebels and contemporary "hoochies" represent a deviant Black female sexuality. The image of jezebel originated under slavery when Black women were portrayed as being ..."sexually aggressive wet nurses" (Clarke et al. 1983, 99). Jezebel's function was to relegate all Black women to the category of sexually aggressive women, thus providing a powerful rationale for the widespread sexual assaults by White men typically reported by Black slave women (Davis 1981; White 1985). Jezebel served another function. If Black slave women could be portrayed as having excessive sexual appetites, then increased fertility should be the expected outcome" (2000, p. 81).*

"Sapphire" stems from a 1920's radio program that evolved into the most popular television program of its time. Two White actors portrayed two Black men who migrated from the south to Chicago. The show's popularity soared once it moved to television and the name changed to *Amos and Andy*. With the introduction of the "Kingfish" character, Sapphire was born and a dominating stereotype was established (Hine, Brown, & Terborg-Penn, 1994a, p. 1009).

> *Sapphire – "As the Kingfish's domineering wife, Sapphire embodied many of the most prevalent stereotypes about African-American women as overbearing, bossy, sharp-tongued, controlling, and emasculating. The most memorable scenes of their marriage consisted of Sapphire scolding the Kingfish, especially about his dishonesty, laziness, and unreliability. Amos 'n' Andy reinforced notions about problematic relationships between Black men and women and sketched an indelible portrait of the stereotypical domineering Black woman in the psyches of Black and white Americans. Sapphire would become ... an acceptable and unquestioned term for so-called emasculating Black women. Sapphire also became a pervasive image in the folk culture of African-Americans and one of the most damaging and pervasive stereotypes of Black women, which still has currency in contemporary conceptions of Black womanhood"*
>
> *(Hine, Brown, & Terborg-Penn, 1994a, pp. 1009-1010).*

Collins (2000) describes the "welfare Mama" as another one of the controlling images used to portray Black women. She ties the welfare mother image to the period of enslavement when Black women and their bodies were co-opted to sustain the industry of slavery.

> *"At its core, the image of the welfare mother constitutes a class-specific, controlling image developed for poor working-class Black women .... Essentially an updated version of the breeder woman image created during slavery, this image provides an ideological justification for efforts to harness Black women's fertility to the needs of a changing political economy. During slavery, the breeder woman image portrayed Black women as more suitable for having children than White women. By claiming that Black women were able to produce children as easily as animals, this image*

> *provided justification for interference in enslaved Africans' reproductive lives. Slave owners wanted enslaved Africans to "breed" because every child born represented a valuable unit of property, another unit of labor, and, if female, the prospects for more slaves"* (2000, p. 78).

Each day we are written into existence through an active narrative that was here when we arrived. The professor in the elevator likely pictured Barbara as the "Welfare Mama." The bank executive saw Jerelyn and probably conjured visions of "jezebel." The man in the club most likely viewed Ebony as a "jezebel" as well. The new mayor probably saw a likeness of the "mammy" in Joyce while she worked at City Hall. For me, each of these images promotes a racialized, gendered script for Black women.

Hegemony dictates that Black women play out these archetypes everyday. According to Omi and Winant (1994), one of the first things people notice when they initially meet someone is the person's race, along with their gender. "Our ability to interpret racial meanings depends on preconceived notions of a racialized social structure" (1994, p. 59). They state that we as a society use race to provide clues about *who* a person is, and are genuinely pained when we can't lump them conveniently into our prescribed category; for example, all Black women fit one hegemonic archetype. Thus, the training participant, the corporate banker, the guy in the club, the college professor and my staff person were all operating from preconceived notions of archetypes ascribed to Black women. Their remarks were generated by a script they were taught about the *group* Black women, regardless of who we are individually.

The racialized, gendered script embodied in these archetypes is also couched in class status. These four foundational archetypes – Mammy, Jezebel, Sapphire, and Welfare Mama – are all positioned at the working class or poor socioeconomic strata, as depicted by Cushner et al (2003). The dominant society is not the sole anticipator of these caricatures. Black people have internalized these archetypes into the culture, as revealed by Barbara and Ebony's experiences. They also expect one of these archetypes to show up when a Black woman enters the room. These prototypes of Black women are branded by how race, gender and class have been mixed into our own social dynamic. Stephens & Phillips (2005) assert that these foundational images are influential frameworks of African American female sexuality, even today.

> *"This is exemplified by the similar, yet more sexually explicit, sexual scripts available today identified by Stephens & Few (2005a), those being the Diva, Gold Digger, Freak, Dyke, Gangsta Bitch, Sister Savior, Earth Mother, and Baby Mama" (2005, p. 39).*

I agree with Stephens & Phillips. These new images are all derivatives of the original archetypes, extended and played out for the sake of pop culture. The authors attribute these modern-day scripts to the gender and racial stereotypes society uses to reference African American adolescent females in the context of the hip-hop culture. What I find fascinating is the omission of "the Trophy" as an archetype for Black women, while it is frequently ascribed to White women in U.S. culture. This is another situation where what would seem a positive for Black women appears simultaneously to be a negative.

"Trophy" is often understood as another term for "gold digger." Barbara took a business trip to Italy during the study. When she returned, study participants queried her about what she saw during the trip and what the experience was like. One thing of particular note was the proliferation of young Black women partnered with older Italian men, an accepted occurrence in Italy that doesn't raise eyebrows. This sparked a discussion of the "trophy." As mentioned before, it is not included as one of the foundational images ascribed to Black women, despite the common use of the term.

A "trophy" is defined as "the spoils of war, dedicated in classical antiquity with an inscription to a deity and set up as a temporary monument on or near a battlefield" (American-Heritage, 2005).

Maschner and Reedy-Maschner (2007), in the abstract description of their chapter on Amerindians and their treatment of trophies, characterize trophies as "symbols of successes in interpersonal violence and warfare" (2007, p. 32). They further typify trophies as synonymous with striving for status and prestige. The authors identify three types of "highly visible trophies" for this population: body parts of victims, women and material items of victims. They say the three categories are interchangeable relative to the status they confer on the victor (p. 32).

I can easily understand the Black woman's exclusion from consideration as a trophy, in the purest sense. The auction block was not a pedestal. Her portrayal in media has never positioned her as someone to be revered. "The way in which black women are perceived in American society – the predominant image is that of the "fallen" woman, the whore, the slut, the prostitute" (hooks, 1981, p. 52). Every foundational image ascribed to Black women in this society is negative, as evidenced in earlier discussion.

A "trophy" is something to be achieved, something to be won. The Black woman, in her position at the "mule of the world" is not seen as a trophy. Black girls born and raised in the United States come to recognize and learn these racialized, gendered scripts as she navigates her lifeworld. Often these scripts are playing out in her home, right before her eyes, as Barbara reflects

> *"When I look at what's tradition, it's really women being subservient. My mother didn't work. My father doled out money to her. She'd sit there and penny-pinch and ... [Jerelyn – she managed]. Yes, but she was beholding to him."*
>
> *Barbara*

These scripts are presented to her everywhere she looks, subliminally and directly. If she exactly follows the script, she accomplishes the performance desired by society.

Performance

> *"Unless you want to get into a big activist battle, you accept the stereotypes given to you and just try and reshape them along the way. So in a way, this gives me a lot of freedom. I can't be looked at any worse in society than I already am – black and female is pretty high on the list of things not to be"*
>
> *(Carroll 1997, 94-95). (Collins, 2000, p. 27)*

"*Performing Black girl*" in concert with society's defined script will lead to "*performing Black woman.*" Racialized, gendered performance is structured through hegemonic archetypes that are fortified via ISAs. Often, like the script, the performance is reinforced through clothing. The internalization of keeping place shows up especially in how we raise our children. Barbara recalls responses she received when she forbade party guests from gifting her then-toddler daughter a Barbie doll for her birthday:

> *"The reaction of people to 'no Barbie' was "what are you growing, a freak?" ... [I understood] that pink symbolized you were prohibited from doing other things. I was really hell-bent on she wasn't going to be prohibited from doing whatever she wanted to do by saying this is the only thing that you could do. It was hard railing against that because people's perceptions were if you're a girl these are the things [type of gifts] you get."*

Performing your assigned script serves to reinforce gender and class roles introduced through the family, education, and church ISAs. Whether its hair style or texture, skin tone, "being uppity", or how you dress – stand apart from the crowd and ISAs will respond. The type of reaction Barbara received was directly related to society's "keeping place" mindset for girls. Cushner et al (2003) offer that socialization is described in three parts:

a) "The child learns to *distinguish* between men and women, and between boys and girls, and to know what kinds of behavior are characteristic of each.
b) The child learns to express appropriate gender role *preferences* for himself or herself.
c) The child learns to *behave* in accordance with gender role standards[15]" (2003, p. 291).

Gender role performance is especially connected to societal dress codes.

Garber (1997) states that dress codes were initiated in Europe "to regulate who wore what, and on what occasion" (p. 20). She says that the codes were initially imposed to discipline the belief that you are what you wear and that clothing sublimated a pecking order. "Your submission to those rules signified your acceptance of your position within the hierarchy" (1997, p. 22). Garber posits that Queen Elizabeth used dress codes to enforce class status in the 1500's. Specific colors and clothing signals set apart dignitaries and commoners "from earls and countesses to gentlemen's wives and men with income of 500 marks" (p. 26).

For women in US society, one aspect of gender performance is relative to appearance. For Ebony's generation, jeans and pants are a way of life with little gender-role consequences. She is fascinated that this hasn't always been the case for women in US society. Jerelyn elaborates, "There was no reason to wear pants; ladies didn't wear pants. When it comes to acting ladylike, ladies wore dresses; and you were a *little lady*, in training!"

Garber offers that gender performance via clothing is usually a subset of class, status, rank or wealth as further associated with either the subordination or the commodification of women (1997, p. 23). She says class designation through dress codes continued into modern society. I support Garber's thoughts that class creates a "pecking order" which I liken to opportunities of "exclusion and inclusion."

15 Cushner et al attribute this to Lenore J. Weitzman, "Sex-Role Socialization," in *Women: A Feminist Perspective*, ed. Jo Freeman (Palo Alto, CA: Mayfield, 1975), p. 109.

This showed up with particular regard to being accepted, being liked by others or being like others. Barbara shared her memory of learning about Jack and Jill, a social organization in "colored culture," as her mother called it:

> *"My mother's friend Mrs. Green had told her about Jack and Jill and invited her to join. She said all the kids around here are members and her mother thought it would be nice for her and her brother to be a part of. A few months later she overheard Mrs. Green tell her mother, "Well to tell the truth when you live in this neighborhood, your kids are wonderful but membership has problems with foreigners; they don't think you'll fit into the group which is central to the organization. I'm so sorry."*

Because her mother is not accepted by the parent group, Barbara and her brother were unable to join Jack and Jill. She concludes, "I think ... we get so caught up with believing that it [exclusion] is only about race and I think what this little scenario speaks to is that *within race* there is exclusion."

Study participants all agree with Barbara's assertion that,

> *"[exclusion is a] whole group experience. It continues to reinforce itself among a cadre of people who feel that, no matter where they are, they are ... they have this right, ability to say 'I can be in something that you can't [reach].'"*

It is my opinion that exclusion and inclusion are by-products of socioeconomic class, an intangible system that presumes access because of economic power. Often this is connected to skin tone, where light skin equals access to benefits:

> *Joyce: "The purpose and the mission of a lot of those elite social organizations are really good. The problem comes with dividing the status of the individuals from what the mission of the organization is."*

Ruth: "That whole light skin, dark skin thing jumps up in sororities all the time."

Barbara: "When I went to Howard for undergraduate school, they had the "paper-bag" test. If you were darker than a paper bag, then you couldn't be in a sorority. [Jerelyn and Ebony have never heard of this and express shock] That's the way it was; it determined who you married, who you dated.

Ruth: "It changes by geographical location; in one state it's the pink-and-green ones that are light and the red-and-white ones are dark; you go to another state and it flips."

Barbara: "At FAMU, that's the first thing they ask you: where'd you go to school; what did you pledge and what church do you belong to?"

Ruth: "I don't know if it's still in practice; but the paper bag test was the litmus test for belonging to a church in Charleston [SC]."

Jerelyn: "Belonging to a church?!"

Ruth: "Yes, that and the "doorjamb" test; if you were darker than the doorjamb, you could not enter."

Livesay (1989), in discussing Giddens (1976) structuration theory, asserts that "systems *have* structures, that is, sets of generative rules and resources which social agents draw upon and instantiate in practice" (1989, p. 265). The women who composed the parent group of Jack and Jill imposed their rules upon the process of membership that supported their preference for who gained access through invitation, and who did not, as did practitioners of the "paper bag" and "doorjamb" tests.

Many people assume that if we all "pull ourselves up by our bootstraps" the world will be a better place. Omi & Winant (1994), in their "Bootstraps model" (p. 21) refute this thinking because the notion requires ethnic people of color to modify themselves and accommodate to societal "norms" or hegemonic notions as defined by the dominant culture. I believe this model is further flawed for two reasons. 1) United States society operates on the same intangible preferences, defined as differing levels of class status, that creates economic separation; and 2) The model assumes equal access to goods and services for everyone. A social justice colleague and I used to joke that one must first have boots in order to pull oneself up by the proverbial bootstraps.

Jerelyn connects clothing to gender performance when she relates her experience in corporate banking. She explains that dress codes for women were restrictive. "It was 1975 when we were allowed to wear pantsuits, and they had to be *a suit*; the jacket had to cover your buttocks." Barbara also encountered professional dress code boundaries for women in the courtroom. "When I first started [law school] classes in 1980, there were judges who would not let you in their courtroom if you didn't wear dresses; if you wore a red dress, they'd go off, calling you a strumpet." Barbara and I, living in different parts of the country, were introduced to dress codes through our elementary experience in Catholic schools. "I went to Catholic school and we couldn't wear pants. No pants, no tights; we wore long socks and I grew up in New York ... it would be cold and you'd have to stand outside in the cold."

Performance prompts the question, *Are we who we think we are or are we who society reflects that we are?* Dorinne Kondo (1997) asserts, "performative citations are the product of constitutive constraints that create identities, creative performances elicited under duress" (Kondo, 1997, p. 7). I interpret this to mean that gender role structure influences performance; for the Black woman this becomes a *contested performance*. Every piece of her appearance is questioned – her skin tone, her hairstyle, and often her clothing, especially when perceived as out of her assigned class level.

> *"A boss once wrote in my evaluation I had 'delusions of grandeur' [Barbara – "you're not supposed to be but so much."] She said I walked into the bank like I owned it. ["Huh" and chuckles among the group: maybe you should have owned it.] And she knew how much money I made, so it was like 'Where do you shop? How do you afford these clothes?' This is a White woman saying this; it was during a time when I rotated among different work groups. The evaluation that they gave me, I could tell that they sat down in a conference room and had a discussion about me."*
>
> *Jerelyn*

Jerelyn's reflection supports the notion that the Black woman's performance *and presentation* are suspect. Deviating from her expected performance indicates she is either being "uppity" or "so articulate" in the dominant society. Among Black culture, she might be accused of "talking white" or not being "Black enough." Race, gender and class dictate the Black woman's scripted performance. Her performance and appearance area constantly being challenged via hegemonic archetypes.

Butler (1990) describes the process of subject formation as one of "performativity" where *enacting* identities bring these identities into being, rather than expressing some predetermined essence. This brings us full circle to Lewin's theory that b*ehavior* is a *function* of the *person* in the e*nvironment*. Lewin's *environment* and Kondo's *constitutive constraints* appear to align: external influences initiate performance, thus creating identities. Butler's theory aligns with Lewin's as well, asserting that we bring life to the identity we are born into; we *perform* the role, for our defined place in society. Omi and Winant (1994) conclude that race is not a biological given but rather a socially constructed way of differentiating human beings (p. 65).

Butler (1990) maintains that gender is identity constructed over time, evolved from the repetition of assigned acts (p. 277). What does this mean for Black girls born and raised in the United States?

My estimation is that Black girls in the United States are socially constructed to follow a racialized, gendered script that is informed by the container of "collective consciousness." Following this script reproduces social formation through interactions in the subordinant[16] and dominant cultures of US society to achieve assimilation, as we'll see in the next section.

Assimilation

> *"Assimilation is the magic in the American dream ... magic helps us become better, more beautiful creatures...[the]American dream of assimilation helps us become the kind of Americans we seek to be. Just conform, the dream whispers, and you will be respected, protected, accepted."*
>
> *(Yoshino, 2006, p. 20)*

Recounting her first visit to a Black beauty shop at age nine, Jerelyn shared how her expectations of leaving with a "Shirley Temple" [hairstyle] were dashed by the shop's owner who gave her the same "pigtails and bangs" style bestowed on every little Black girl. Some of the women apparently had spoken to her mother before about her special hairstyle:

> *"Why are you going to have this "white girl" hairdo? When are you going to get this child to look like other Black children? She is a Black child; it's bad enough that she acts different, she has to assimilate here."*
>
> *Jerelyn*

Assimilation is the tool of internalized oppression used for keeping [you in your assigned] place. It is a tool used in both the dominant culture and the Black community. Barbara with her close cropped

16 Barbara Love (2000) coined the term "subordinant" as a more direct parallel with "dominant"; both are nouns used here. She suggests "dominate" be used along with "subordinate"; both are adjectives that describe what's being done (p. 474).

curly natural hair and Ruth with her natural locks push the hairstyle envelope everyday. Jerelyn states firmly, "it's about assimilation; we can assimilate in pretty much every way into the majority culture with the exception of our color and our hair. The fact that you rebel in your dress, in your hair is too much blackness." Thanks to the notion of 'keeping place" we struggle for acceptance in the dominant society and within our own Black culture.

We will never truly earn the respect, protection or acceptance Yoshino mentions. Our Black community expects us to "straighten that hair;" accuses us of "being uppity," "talking white," and/ or performing "too much like White folks." Any of these clearly indicates you are moving out of your place. As the group discusses, Black women have always had a defined place:

> *Ruth: "In When and Where I Enter she discusses Black women's role in the political process and in the SNCC movement and how they were treated ..."*
>
> *Barbara: "Make the coffee and run the copies 'cause that's all you're good for. We'd like to think it's really changed, but it hasn't. Women are still not heading corporations; they let us in yet still not let us in."*

According to Yoshino (2006), "covering" is about making Whites feel comfortable. We are assured that being analogous to the dominant culture is impossible (Brent, 1973; Collins, 2000; Genovese, 1976; Giddings, 2001; Woodson, 1933). The dominant culture expects assimilation – to *do* white although we'll never actually *be* white.

Gender assimilation is pushed upon us as well. Jerelyn and Barbara were directed to be consistent with the pre-defined role set forth for women in our society. Jerelyn's mother attempted to break her independent streak by admonishing, "It's gonna take you longer to get married." Barbara is resistant to this push as well, as she adamantly states below:

> *"The other thing is the expectation that's what we're supposed to be like. I was never told I couldn't do anything and now my father is saying 'they'll bring me back'; my mother is saying I need to get ready to learn [to be a wife] and I railed against it. I never thought of myself as having to become a wife; only to be a lawyer like [my favorite uncle] Ton-Ton Pierre."*

From the time we are born, we are acculturated to perform girl. Subtle messages come through the ISAs as we mature: girls play with dolls, learn to cook, and play house; we're expected to get married, and raise a family. Over twenty years ago, one of my college dorm mates said her parents sent her to school to find a husband; that script is still in place today, in the 21st century. My goddaughter recently became engaged while completing her masters program. Among the congratulatory comments at her graduation I heard, "She graduated and found a good man, *too.*"

Another aspect of assimilationist culture in the United States specific to the Black community is "the dozens," a game of insults carried out in a teasing manner. "From Giddayup, the insult game would have been played in the slave communities, eventually taking on the English name, "the dozens" (Smitherman, 1999, p. 225). One origin cites enslaved Africans in the New World connecting to their remembered cultural practices and verbal rituals from several cultures in Africa. These remembrances helped them adapt to life in a strange new land. Smitherman posits the dozens offered oppressed people an outlet for "laughing to keep from crying."

According to Smitherman, the dozens was a form of release for the suppressed rage and frustrations resulting from being a Black man or woman trapped in White America. The dozens taught discipline and self-control, and was a lesson in survival using verbal wit and cunning rhetoric (1999, p. 225). She identifies sophisticated rules of the game: fundamentally that the players know each other and that males and females only played in same-sex, intimate settings (1999, p. 227).

Smitherman says the insults usually focused on a person's mother and on occasion, extended to include fathers, grandmothers and other familial members. According to Smitherman, moving beyond this topic indicated crossing the line or increasing the level of insult. It is particularly stinging when the insults refer to one's mother.

I'm more familiar with another origin for the dozens that Smitherman mentions. It refers to the devaluing on the auction block of enslaved men and women who were aged, past their prime, injured and infirm after years of backbreaking toil, and no longer were capable of hard labor. These enslaved human beings often were assembled in lots of a dozen in hopes of fetching a fair market price (1999, p. 225). Smitherman discussed the game as a premise for survival – a mechanism transported from ancestral Africa. What I find disturbing is how it was suitable to diminish Black women in some African cultures; moreover, how it is historically acceptable to devalue Black women here in United States culture.

I agree with Yoshino's (2006) assertion that assimilation is about making Whites feel comfortable. According to Smitherman (1999), it is nearly commonplace for this game of insults – originally confined to "the hood" – to be played in the general public, beyond the parameters of friends and family. We are now accustomed to Black comedians and entertainers engaging "the dozens" in their performances. I contend it is this type of familiarity that led to the radio announcer engaging the phrase "nappy headed hos." He believed that its presence in the cultural milieu made it acceptable for him to utter those words. I argue that he also believed, as a member of the dominant society, that his external view of Black culture allowed him a commentator status that gave him license to the phrase.

Because of this one-sided comfort, I believe the dominant culture feels a false familiarity that leads them to say anything about and do anything to Black women.

> *"I was a young girl just out of college, worked in trust accounting and wanted to become a trust officer; a position*

became open. One of the trust officers came down the hall: "Miss Andrews, I understand you are applying for such-and-such position. I just want to tell you, you are the sexiest young thing." I just looked at him and tried to contain myself to keep from slapping the mess out of him, 'cause I was very militant in those days. I guess the look on my face told him he'd cross over the line. He said, "Are you surprised?" I said no, it is very common for a man not to know the proper thing to say to a lady; that is inappropriate, and I don't appreciate it. "I just ..." There is nothing you can say, other than to apologize to me. I was shaking, I was upset, but I was angry enough to let him know that he had crossed over the line."

Jerelyn

Writing this makes me recognize that I hold conflicting thoughts about "the dozens." I can appreciate the skill exhibited by those who play the game; and have sometimes been envious of this ability. Yet, I am bothered by the continued ridicule of Black people, particularly Black women, in Black culture and on the public stage. The radio announcer, the trust officer - as Jerelyn says, "They don't always know what to say, [they] have no boundaries, [they] don't stay within appropriateness, and are disrespectful." In Black culture, there is questioning of what is perceived as breaking the cycle of sameness, as Barbara demonstrates:

"It's also you're different; what makes you think you can be different? That's the other message I think we send – 'Who do you think you are that you just gonna walk around [looking, being different?]' How do you do that [with your hair]? What do you put in your hair to get it like that? People have this thing that you're supposed to look a certain way."

Jerelyn's earlier comment regarding Black women's ability to assimilate in every way except our skin color and hair is an interesting notion. Bleaching cream products are still available in my local drug store. We keep beauty shops in business by filling their chairs regularly to get 'perms' – chemical treatments that will get us "good hair" (Bonner, 1991). From my visual scan of the culture, permanent hairstyles are prevalent for Black women entering corporate America and those aspiring to do so. I think the ISAs have become so ingrained that many of us follow the hegemonic push to assimilate; but at what cost?

Resistance & Resilience: Mah Soul Look Back and Wondah How Ah Got Ovah (read as Gullah)

> *"The way I look at it, a white person might be judging me, but I'm judging them, too. If they seem as if they was scornful of a colored person, at the same time that they was scornful of me, I'm the same way about them... if my place ain't good enough for you – [if] I ain't good enough to drink out of a glass that you got because I'm black, I don't want to do it." Sara Brooks, in Simonsen, 1986, p.199*
>
> *(Collins, 2000, p. 201)*

"*How Ah Got Ovah (How I Got Over)*" is the title of an old Negro spiritual whose lines came to mind as I prepared to write this section. During my NCCJ Dismantling Racism retreat experience, participants were separated into cultural affinity groups for several activities. One of the questions posed to the group of Black women and men during an early affinity group session is, "What do you love about being Black?" The words "resistance and resilience" were uttered multiple times around the circle; we spoke about the fact that, no matter what, we keep on keepin' on." It's like something in our spirits refuse to let Black people in this culture stop even when barriers deter our progress.

> *"If anything it pushes you to take those extra steps because sometimes you have to. If it's between me and a girl the same age, educational background, same qualifications for a job, I know that I'd have to still push myself a lot harder than she'd have to in order to get where I need to go. I think that might be part of it."*
>
> *Ebony*

Ebony's comment is a good depiction of resistance which is defined as "the inherent ability of an organism to resist harmful influences" (Merriam-Webster, 2007) or "a process in which the ego opposes the conscious recall of anxiety-producing experiences" (American-Heritage, 2000). Merriam-Webster characterizes resilience as "the capability of a strained body to recover its size and shape after deformation caused especially by compressive stress" and "the ability to recover from or adjust easily to misfortune or change" (2007). As I consider these descriptions, an audible "huh" escapes my lips. I recalled the experiences the women shared in the pilot and research study sessions; and the writings of Black female authors crossed my mind – resistance and resilience indeed. All the women that I encountered bore witness to Black women's ability to resist harmful influences and our capacity to reshape ourselves, and recover from historic incidences of misfortune and the compressive stresses of this society, as Barbara shows in this reflection:

> *"My grandfather was a journalist who spoke out and was eventually murdered. My grandmother had four children; the oldest was 19 and the youngest 12 or something. She basically pulled those kids through and did what needed to be done. How do you say 'no' to your children? How do you go 'I'm so weak, I can't handle it? What do you mean 'you can't handle it?' no one else can do it for them but you! It's not like there's an option; even if you have a strong fam-*

ily, there was still something very personal about them doing what they needed to do."

Barbara

Resistance: I'm A Survivor!

Collins (2000) asserts that, "historically African-Americans' resistance to racial and class oppression could not have occurred without an accompanying struggle for group survival" (2000, p. 201). She further defines this "struggle for survival" as a form of Black women's resistance, and names two primary dimensions of women's activism that demonstrate survivalist behavior: actions taken to create Black female spheres of influence within existing social structures and struggles for institutional transformation. These include efforts to change discriminatory policies and procedures in the institutions that provide the underpinning for our society (2000, p. 204).

A few notable Black women resistors include Mary McLeod Bethune - founder of Bethune Cookman College; Ida B. Wells - journalist and anti-lynching crusader; Anna Julia Cooper, critical intellectual who inspired the works of W.E.B. DuBois and Roy Wilkins; Vashti Murphy McKenzie, first ordained female bishop in the A. M. E. Church; and Dorothy Height, President of the National Council of Negro Women. Each of these women used/uses influence, intelligence and internal fortitude to change the social structure in her spheres of influence. I contend that "resistance" for Black women in the United States constitutes rejecting hegemonic archetypes of who the dominant society says we should be.

Joyce: "There was a situation in adult life where I was being treated 'colored' so how you handle it makes a difference. Everything I did in that office had to be <u>above</u> what everyone else did in order to prove myself."

Barbara: "So a Black girl has to do 400% ..."

> *Ruth: "I agree Barbara; it really is 400%. If you put my Black self and my female self and all that goes into ... maybe that's what makes a Strong Black Woman. When I walk out of my house, on any given day I'm dealing with two different perspectives or two different sets of judgments that hit me when I walk in the door."*

Sometimes resistance is toward family when it comes to breaking with the script, as Barbara and Jerelyn both did. Barbara instills this spirit in her daughter by constantly reaffirming in her "you can be anything you want, play with anything you want – you can do anything." Ebony exemplifies this learned trait from her mother: "Personally I am [resistant to gender stereotypes] because of the way I was raised. My mother made sure I had a variety of things to play with – dolls, various learning toys, and things like that."

Each of the research participants resonated with lessons of picking ourselves up and moving on. Ruth says that following a spiritual and emotional beating she suffered at a previous employer, her mother asked "[Are] you gonna lay in that all day or are you going to do something? This doesn't define you; you don't stay right there where that is; it happened. You keep moving beyond it." Jerelyn shares an observation of how we all benefit from this characteristic:

> *"In each one of the stories I heard, I didn't hear that it made you less of a person. You may have felt bad about that individual experience, but you still came out of it okay. We didn't let it define us; we accepted that this was part of the growth process."*

Shorter-Gooden (2004), in her study of African American women's coping strategies, pinpoints internal resources, an external resource and specific coping strategies for resisting the dual oppressions of racism and sexism. *Internal resources* are particular to the emotional context from which a woman responds and often guide her choice of a specific coping response (2004, p. 416). These include *resting on faith*, prayer and relationship with God to cope with challenges of being Black and female; *standing on shoulders*, a connection to heritage and the ancestors; and *valuing oneself*, loving, respecting and feeling good about oneself, and working hard not to take in society's negative stereotypes about Black women (pp. 416-417). She names *leaning on shoulders* as the *external resource*; this has to do with "relying on resources outside of oneself" which constitutes developing and using social support to cope with the stress brought on by racial and gender bias (p. 417). While the external resource and internal resources appear to be constantly in use, Shorter-Gooden posits other tactics a Black woman can call upon, as needed, to manage the dailyness of oppression.

She identifies *specific coping strategies* as tactics used for managing situational bias. First of these is *role flexing*, altering one's self and appearance to fit in with the dominant group. This motivation to alter looks or appearance may also be described as *proving them wrong* in order to disprove negative stereotypes (p. 418). Next is *avoiding*, staying away from people, situations, or discussion topics likely to stir up biases or prejudices. Third, she identifies *standing up and fighting back* as refusing to role flex or capitulate in any manner by actively fighting back (pp. 419-420).

In Table II below, I parallel Shorter-Gooden's (2004) resources with Harris's (1992) cultural model for growth and development. Harris's *sense of identity* – self-perception and self-knowledge – aligns with Shorter-Gooden's *valuing oneself.*

TABLE 2. BLACK WOMEN'S TOOLS FOR RESISTANCE[17]

Shorter-Gooden (2004)	Harris (1992)	Resource/Strategy
Standing on Shoulders Leaning on Shoulders	Sense of Belonging	Connection to family Cultivated Relationships
Valuing Oneself	Sense of Identity	Self-Perception Self-Knowledge
Resting on Faith Coping Strategies	Sense of Control	Prayer, Relationship w/ God Adapt, Avoid, Fight back

Similarly, Harris's *sense of belonging* – interdependence and being connected – lines up with *standing on shoulders*, and I would link it to *leaning on shoulders*. The former relates to resources associated through heritage while the latter is generated via external resources beyond one's family of origin. Shorter-Gooden's *resting on faith* and *specific coping strategies* relate to Harris's *sense of control* – the attempt to be fully in command of what happens in one's own life in the context of an oppressive society.

According to Bell & Nkomo's (1998) notion of *armoring*, families transfer these qualities via the *sense of belonging* they instill in their daughters. This *sense of belonging* aligns with Harris's (1992) model as well, supporting Shorter-Gooden's (2004) internal resources. Gibbs (2003) identifies the roles of religion and family as two of four major cultural values African American families use as "adaptive responses to their historical and social experiences in American society" (2003, pp. 100-101). Part of Black women's socialization is guiding their daughters in how to adapt and perform effectively outside their communities of culture. While resistance shows up via the above qualities, I believe resilience becomes evident in the persona of the "Strong Black Woman."

17 Black Women's Tools for Resistance. Copyright 2008, R. D. Edwards.

Resilience, Generational Memory & the Strong Black Woman

> *"The social systems in which structure is recursively implicated comprise the situated activities of human agents, reproduced across time and space."*
>
> *(Giddens, 1984, p. 25)*

When I first mentioned the phrase *Strong Black Woman (SBW)* to study participants, everyone knew what I meant. The phrase required no explanation. We each see/have seen this characteristic in our mothers, grandmothers, sister-friends and other Black women we know. Each of us agreed that it could be a negative, particularly when used as a way of oppressing or diminishing Black women. The phrase is a cultural phenomenon that we recognize yet are challenged to define.

> *"It's just in there; I couldn't tell you how. What I don't know is how not to because that's not in my DNA. I saw my mother do it; she saw her mother do it. We don't know how not to be strong Black women." Ruth*

Greene quotes Spencer (1987) saying, "A Black child's preparation by parents and other socializing agents to understand and take pride in her own culture can be a major source of resilience and coping; and that its absence leaves a Black child at additional risk for impaired development" (1990, p. 217). Greene's assertion of impaired development is the outcome I propose for Black girls who don't have access to Gibb's aforementioned cultural values. For these girls the world is _____. I have long held the belief that the lessons learned from enslavement somehow transcend history and inform our thinking today as Black women. During the 'awareness of being Black' aspect of the study, Barbara first mentioned the idea of *collective consciousness* relative to "knowing place." This is in concert with Wilson's (1978) concept of "group conscious". Barbara raised the idea of conscious knowledge shared across generations - what I call *generational memory* in the follow-up dialogue.

> *"The memory thing that you talk about; if you think generationally ... as each generation comes up ... if you think of it as a river and we're like little tributaries off that river. Something seeps through that river into those tributaries of memory and perhaps a lot of the stuff we have now is really – the woman not being able to be dependent on the man and all the rest of that – perhaps that has seeped into our collective consciousness as we go from generation to generation."*

Barbara's reference to "the woman not being able to be dependent on the man" has to do with a control tactic of slaveholders credited to the aforesaid Willie Lynch (1712) speech. Study participants discussed the notion of a "frozen independent state;" and believe it would have socialized Black women not to depend on anyone, particularly Black men. During enslavement there was no guarantee a Black man would be available at the end of the day; he could be killed or sold at the whim of the master (Brent, 1973). There was no "knight in shining armor" for the enslaved African woman; in our experience, it is rare that one shows up for today's contemporary Black woman. This maintains the idea of the SBW – Strong Black Woman.

Juanita Johnson-Bailey (2003) asserts, "If you asked an African American woman how she gets by in a world that is often hostile toward her, she is likely to say that she's just "strong" or that she "just does what she has to do" (p. 82). Each of the women in the study considers herself an SBW. When pressed to answer how they believe this evolved, they generate similar responses without uncovering a definitive answer:

> *"We're asked, 'How did/do you do it?' You do it because you don't have a choice. When people say to us as Black women, 'How'd you do that? How did you get past that?' You pick yourself up and take care of those children and*

you do what you're supposed to do. You don't sit there and wallow, 'Oh my God, oh my God', you just do it. You get fortitude from somewhere and you do it." Barbara

"[It's] connected with the fact that it's how we made it through slavery times; you had to show strength to overcome bondage; in marriage situations, show strength to keep family together in spite of whatever comes; in school and in workplace, show that 'I'm strong enough to deal with this.'" Joyce

"Personally I am that way because of the way I was raised; my father is in my life but, in terms of being an active parent, he just provides. My mother was the one who held the final word." Ebony

Regarding how our foremothers did it: "It's not like there's an option; even if you have strong family support [there was] still something very personal about them doing what they needed to do."

Barbara

These quotes support my contention that the "Strong Black Woman" is socially constructed through generational memory from the Black women who preceded us. I consider *generational memory* to be in concert with Haug's (1987) collective memory.

Haug sees collective memory as a "tool individuals use to construct themselves" (1987, p. 33). Rupert Sheldrake (1995) suggests that memory is inherent in nature and that it informs a historical process of social construction. Sheldrake says that human societies and cultures have characteristic patterns resulting from stable, well-established social and cultural structures from the past. He further asserts that we all inherit memory from people who are like us, that precede us, no matter how long ago they existed(1995, p. 240). According to Sheldrake, these structures stand strong despite the continual cycle of population change through death and birth because each society incorporates individuals into social groups and orients them to how things are done.

I believe Black girls are shaped by their culture of familiars before being exposed to broader societal institutions. Greene (1990) supports this when she contends that

> *"Black mothers must prepare their daughters to become Black women. They must communicate the racial and sexual dangers and realities of the world that confront Black women, how to make sense of them, when and how to respond to racial dangers if at all. It may be incumbent on Black mothers to provide more positive messages and alternatives (to white middle class ideal) to their daughters to offset the negative reflections they see of themselves in the eye of the dominant culture" (1990, p. 218).*

If imparted successfully, a Black girl is well-armed to resist racialized, gendered scripting and performance.

Johnson-Bailey (2003) concurs with Collins (2000) when she asserts that the African American woman's existence is one of resistance. One of the women in her study on Black women and feminism stated, "We have to be strong because of our place in society. We do what we have to do to survive and then we break down and cry." A friend recently remarked that she holds herself together throughout a crisis and when things are set aright, she lets herself [feel the emotion and] cry. I offer this as an example of Shorter-Gooden's (2004) "coping strategies" and Harris's (1992) "sense of control." By controlling her response to circumstances, a Black woman may be fully in control of her world at that moment.

A friend gifted me a framed poem by Maya Angelou that says, "When we cast our bread upon the waters, we can presume that someone downstream whose face we may never see will benefit from our action, even as we enjoy the gifts sent to us from a donor upstream." The ancestors handed down what they knew we needed to function in this culture. Angelou's quote reminds me of Barbara's analogy; generational memory is the river, Black girls and women are the tributaries. The river streams forward allowing us to join it, take what we need, and leave behind tributary gifts for those who follow.

I believe there are historical implications for why we take from the stream. The water is a spiritual and symbolic link to the ancestors. The point of embarkation for the slave trade was from Goreé Island in Senegal on the west coast of Africa. Points of debarkation dotted the Caribbean and the Atlantic coast of the United States from Florida to South Carolina to Virginia to New York. I believe "taking from the stream" metaphorically connects us to the ancestors and back to Africa, the motherland.

Emerging Themes – How Black Girls Become Black Women

Sharing My Sisiters' Thoughts

"Me, woman, feeling powerful inside
Me, woman, when I look around
Me, has become many!!

Fanny
Leslie
Andy
Emma
Bonnie
Jackie
Brenda, Carol B.
Aracelly, Olga, Ceil
Bev, Marge and Bea
Gilda, Fran and Mary

Now, many women, we be feeling powerful inside
All of us...
Mellow, like the fruits we pick in summer
All of us, got some secrets inside
known some pain
a few memories perhaps
of having lost, despite loving hard yesteryear
Minds so powerful

always methodical in our search
for something, someone special
to behold -

Mind powerful women
learning to live alone
with our babies
our bills
and our loneliness

Something special about us
mind powerful women."

Rosemari Mealy

This study is the product of my lifelong curiosity about how Black women came to be the way we are. I began this chapter by speculating about a phenomenon that I noticed in my life experiences and interactions with other Black women. Whether in the Southeast, the Midwest or the South, I noticed that I shared a similar thought pattern with my Black women friends. It appeared to me that we'd all gotten the same messages from cultural proverbs. How could this be when we were not from the same geographical region?

I feel a sense of community with other Black women. Our eyes meet and there is an instant acknowledgement. We smile across a room or nod at one another in passing. I have three sisters by birth; and have acquired cultural sisters in different states where I've lived. I sense that, because of our race and our gender, we share a bond.

Black women born and raised in the United States live in the intersection of race, gender and class. It is the reality of who we are and how society responds to us in the daily course of our existence. How is it that my thinking might mirror that of Black women from other parts of the country? Some answers lay in the theoretical findings of research that's been done on Black girls and Black women. Other answers unfolded as I listened to and analyzed participants' memories and comments.

Additional answers became apparent through the session dialogues I convened and engaged for this study. Black girls in the United States are shaped by the historic experiences of Black women in the US. We navigate this society by moving through and interacting with its institutions, with people of other cultures, with our men and with each other. This history extends back over four hundred years to the initial arrival of Africans to these shores. What did these African queens and princesses do that enabled them to create a source of strength that we tap into over 400 years later?

Africans were forced to acculturate into US culture through the institution of slavery. Hegemony and ideological state apparatus (ISA) facilitated their socialization process through legalized enslavement. Following 200+ years of enslavement, ISAs stepped in to suppress Black people legally by weaving the hegemonic notion of inferiority into its institutions. In the midst of this, a picture of Black women was created and presented her as a creature of multiple myths. She is forced to constantly prove herself an actual woman (White, 1999) in the face of stereotypical archetypes.

Like many Black people, Black women believed the lies told about Black people by the dominant society. They facilitated internalized oppression against one another and other Black folks. However, they also return regularly to the company of their sisters, realizing that safety is inherent in the sense of belonging provided by the group. They embrace the spaces Collins (2000) calls prime locations for resisting objectification as the "Other" because in these spaces Black women realize that the feminine images of the larger culture are unsuitable. Here, they go about the business of fashioning themselves after the historic black female role models of their community (2000, p. 101).

I believe the intrinsic quality of resistance rises to the surface in these spaces. It has always undergirded Black women's existence. The triumvirates of senses – belonging, identity and control – secure Black women's self-image and strengthen their ability to adapt, avoid or fight in the face of oppression. Faith provides a level of strength and assurance. Resilience allows Black women to 'keep on keepin' on' because they are standing on the shoulders of ancestors and surrounded by the Sisters.

Chapter 5: Internalized Collective Consciousness

"My actions ... are the result of the cumulative effect of a lifetime of racial slights and injustices suffered because of my color. God, what it must feel like to go through the day without ever once having to think about my coat of armor."

(Williams, 2000, p. 10)

Internalized Collective Consciousness

Stanley Milgram first proposed the notion that there are "six degrees of separation" potentially linking any two people (Kleinfeld, 2002). I interpret this to mean that somewhere along the way we are all connected. In Black culture, I grew up hearing that if we engaged in conversation with each other long enough, we might find a connection between us. I believe something similar happens with Black women. Wilson (1978) posed the notion of "group consciousness." In our attempt to understand this phenomenon, Barbara and I put forward the terms "collective consciousness" and "generational memory."

As I conclude this research, it seems we need a term to identify what it is that Black women born and raised in the United States share. I offer “Internalized Collective Consciousness” (ICC). “Internalized,” because it is inside us; each of us comes with a “group consciousness” present and ready to be accessed. “Collective” speaks to the meaningful influence of cultural attachment (Thomas 2004) that is apparent only to other Black women through this shared history. This mechanism allows us to access generational lessons and strategies and share them with those who come behind us. “Consciousness” is the container that enables Black women to play a socially defined role through which each contributes to the preservation and advancement of the group (Wilson, 1978, p. 160).

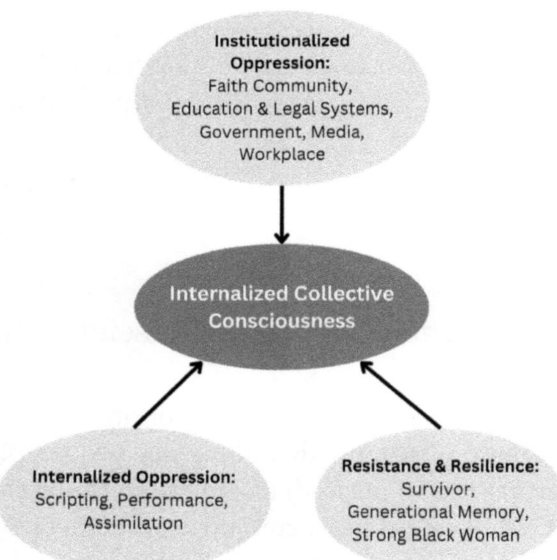

This “Internalized Collective Consciousness” is essential to Black women’s socialization and development in US culture. Their survival strategies were created during enslavement and honed through over 400 years of systemic oppression in U.S. society. By tapping into this ICC, Black women have been able to remain poised while performing the dance Scott (1991) calls the "cultural chorus line." The psychological chains of enslavement remain present in US culture, facilitated by institutionalized subjugation. Black women have utilized ICC to traverse their way among their culture of familiars as well as in the dominant society.

Our collective existence in the systemically oppressed container socialized us to believe that we are our own problem. We acculturated the lies told about Black people and made them our truths. We taught our girls to resist and to fight back, even when it was clear that no one would defend our honor. At our core, it seems the spirits of the ancestors – Harriet, Sojourner, Anna, Jarena – and others compelled us to resist and hark back to our true African selves. The survivor in us pushes forth against the oppressive society.

This proposed framing results from my experience of engaging with seven other Black women to examine our socialization experience in US society. Collaborative inquiry was conducted in a pilot session and a six-week series of full study. We explored our first memories of realizing we were Black and first memories of realizing we were girls. We also examined our first memories of recognizing class difference. We identified class difference by focusing on what we had that others didn't and what others had that we didn't.

We sought to describe and understand how Black girls become Black women in the cultural container of US society. Black girls plot a course to Black womanhood while living at the intersection of race, gender and class. I discovered that Black girls are formed in the triumvirate of senses – belonging, identity and control (Harris, 1992) – instilled by her parents and her culture of familiars. As she matures, she develops coping strategies (Shorter-Gooden, 2004) that enable her to stand on the shoulders of the ancestors and lean on faith as she maintains her forward movement into and through adulthood. These foundational resources facilitate self-esteem and self-definition that prepare her to stand in the face of micro-aggressions and full-on oppression.

In her treatise on the psychology of Black women, Thomas (2004) puts forward seven guiding principles for conducting research on Black women. This study has addressed four of these principles: knowledge development, contextuality, connectedness, and collaboration and cross-fertilization. The study presents new information about Black women born and raised in the United States and offers "a more profound understanding" (2004, p. 297) of who Black women are in this culture. The results reveal connections to their "motivations, attitudes and behaviors relative to individual characteristics" (2004, p. 298) within the context of the micro, meso and macro environments. The research is culturally attached to the psyche of Black women (2004, p. 298). The results were achieved through collaboration with Black women and framed in the context of Black feminist thought, oppression theory, identity development, social construction and the psychology of Black women.

References

Abramovitz, M. (1997). Children, race and power: Kenneth and Mamie Clark's Northside Center. *American Journal of Public Health, 87*(9), 1568-1569.

Althusser, L. (1971). *Lenin and philosophy and other essays*. Retrieved July 9, 2006.

American-Heritage. (2000). The American heritage dictionary of the English language: fourth edition. Retrieved September, 2007, from http://www.bartleby.com

American-Heritage. (2005). The American heritage dictionary of the English language. Retrieved October 12, 2007, from http://www.bartleby.com

Angelou, M. (1994). *The complete collected poems of Maya Angelou* (First ed.). New York: Random House.

Bell, E. L. J. E., & Nkomo, S. (1998). Armoring: learning to withstand racial oppression. *Journal of Comparative Family Studies, 29*(2), 285-295.

Bentz, V. M., & Shapiro, J. J. (1998). *Mindful inquiry in social research*. Thousand Oaks Sage.

Billingsley, A. (1999). *Mighty like a river: the Black church and social reform* (First ed.). New York: Oxford University Press.

Birdsong, M., Branding, R., Colgan, C., Davis, H., Ferguson, M., Gallagher, M. B., et al. (1995). *Building an Inclusive Community Workshop manual.*Unpublished manuscript, St. Louis.

Bonner, L. B. (1991). *Good hair: for colored girls who've considered weaves when the chemicals became too ruff* (First ed.). New York: Crown Publications.

Bowles, S., & Gintis, H. (1976). *Schooling in capitalist America: educational reform and the contradictions of economic life* (First ed.). New York: Basic Books, Inc. .

Brent, L. H. B. J. (1973). *Incidents in the life of a slave girl.* New York: Harcourt Brace Jovanovich.

Bush, G. (2003). Walking the collaborative talk: creating inquiry groups. *Knowledge Quest, 32*(1), 1.

Butler, J. (1990). *Performative acts and gender constitution: an essay in phenomenology and feminist theory*. Baltimore: Johns Hopkins University Press.

Cade, T. (Ed.). (1970). *The Black Woman: an anthology*. New York: Signet, NAL Penguin Inc.

Callero, P. L. (2003). The sociology of the self. *Annual Review of Sociology, 29*, 115-133.

Cohen, B. S., & Hirschkop, P. J. (1967). Loving vs. Virginia (Vol. 388. U.S. 1, pp. 6): FindLaw: Cases and Codes.

Cole, Y. (2006, March). You're so articulate. *Diversity, Inc., 5*, 52-56.

Collins, P. H. (2000). *Black feminist thought: knowledge, consciousness and the politics of empowerment* (Second ed.). New York: Routledge.

Crawford, J., Kippax, S., Onyx, J., Gault, U., & Benton, P. (1992). *Emotion and gender: constructing meaning from memory*. London: SAGE.

Creswell, J. W., & Miller, D. L. (2000). Determining validity in qualitative inquiry. *Theory Into Practice, 39*(3), 124-130.

Cummins, T., Garcia-Ruiz, C., Jackson, R., Nickens, R., Porteous, G., Potapchuk, M., et al. (1994). *Building an Inclusive Community Workshop Manual.* Paper presented at the Building an Inclusive Community, St. Louis, Missouri.

Cummins, T., Harris, C., Mubarak-Tharpe, A., Nickens, J., Rudy , Potapchuk, M., & Sharpe, L. (1996, October 20-25, 1996). *Diversity Resources Manual.* Paper presented at the Dismantling Racism Institute, Alton, Illinois.

Cummins, T., Harris, C., Mubarak-Tharpe, A., Nickens, R., Potapchuk, M., Speed, R., et al. (1996). *Diversity resources manual.*Unpublished manuscript, St. Louis.

Cushner, K., McClelland, A., & Safford, P. (2003). *Human diversity in education: an integrative approach* (4th ed.): McGraw-Hill.

Davis, A. (1981). *Women, race and class.* New York: Vintage Books.

Dodds, J. (1995). Collaborative group inquiry: a blend of research and therapy. *Australian Social Work, 48*(3), 8.

Du Bois, W. E. B. (1969). *The souls of Black folk.* New York: Bantam Books.

Edwards, R. D. (2005). Interrupting structural inequality in the classroom (pp. 81): Fielding Graduate University

Edwards, R. D. (2006). Black church as an organization - Black women in ministry (pp. 54): Fielding Graduate University

Farrar, P. (2001). *Too painful to remember: memory-work as a method to explore sensitive research topics.* Paper presented at the Conference Name|. Retrieved Access Date|. from URL|.

Garber, M. (1997). *Vested interests: cross-dressing and cultural anxiety* (2 ed.). New York: Routledge Paperback Edition.

Genovese, E. D. (1976). *Roll, Jordan, roll: the world the slaves made* (First ed.). New York: Random House, Inc. .

Gibbs, J. T. (2003). African American children and adolescents. In J. T. G. a. L. N. Huang (Ed.), *Children of Color: psychological interventions with culturally diverse youth* (pp. 95-145). San Francisco: Jossey-Bass.

Giddens, A. (1984). *The constitution of society: outline of the theory of structuration* (First paperback - 1986 ed.). Berkeley University of California Press.

Giddings, P. (1984). *When and where I enter: the impact of Black women on race and sex in America* (1st ed.). New York: William Morrow and Company.

Giddings, P. (2001). *When and where I enter: the impact of Black women on race and sex in America* (2nd ed.). New York: HarperCollins.

Goldhaber, D. E. (2000). *Theories of human development: integrative perspectives*. California: Mayfield Publishers.

Green-Fareed, C. (2006). Literature review of the lifeworld of African American women (pp. 33): Fielding Graduate University.

Green, T. (2003). A gendered spirit: race, class and sex in the African American church. *Race, Gender & Class, 10*(1).

Greene, B. (1994). African American women. In L. G. Comas-Diaz, Beverly (Ed.), *Women of color: integrating ethnic and gender identities in psychotherapy* (pp. 10-29). New York: The Guilford Press.

Greene, B. A. (1990). What has gone before: the legacy of racism and sexism in the lives of Black mothers and daughters. *Women and Therapy, 9*, 207-230.

Guidano, V. (1991). *The self in process: toward a post-rationalist cognitive therapy*. New York: The Guilford Press.

Gurira, D. (2001). Black women in psychology (pp. 83): Macalester College.

Hardiman, R., & Jackson, B. W. (1997). Conceptual foundations for social justice courses. In M. Adams, L. Bell & P. Griffin (Eds.), *Teaching for Diversity and Social Justice* (pp. 16-29). New York: Routledge.

Harris, C., & Neal, T. (2002). History of racism matrix. In H. of (Ed.) (pp. 1): The National Conference for Community and Justice Dismantling Racism Institute.

Harris, D. J. (1992). A cultural model for assessing the growth and development of the African American female. *Journal of Multicultural Counseling and Development, 20*, 9.

Haug, F. (1987). *Female sexualization: a collective work of memory*. London: Verso.

Henriques, Z. W. (1995). African American women: the oppressive intersection of gender, race and class. *Women & Criminal Justice,* 7(1), 67-80.

Hine, D. C., Brown, E. B., & Terborg-Penn, R. (Eds.). (1994a). *Black women in America: an historical encyclopedia* (1st ed. Vol. 2). Bloomington, IN: Indiana University Press.

Hine, D. C., Brown, E. B., & Terborg-Penn, R. (Eds.). (1994b). *Black women in America: an historical encyclopedia* (1st ed. Vol. 1). Bloomington, IN: Indiana University Press.

Hoare, C. H. (1991). Psychological identity development and cultural others. *Journal of Counseling & Development,* 70(September/October), 9.

Holtzman, L. (2000). *Media messages: what film, television and popular music teach us about race, class, gender, and sexual orientation* (First ed.). New York: M.E. Sharpe, Inc.

hooks, b. (1981). *Ain't I a woman: Black women and feminism*. Boston: South End Press.

hooks, b. (1989). *Talking back: thinking feminist, thinking black*. Cambridge, MA: South End Press.

hooks, b. (1993). *Sisters of the yam: black women and self-recovery*. Boston: South End Press.

hooks, b. (2000). *Where we stand: class matters*. New York: Routledge.

Johnson-Bailey, J. (2003). Everyday perspectives on feminism: African American women speak out. *Race, Gender & Class, 10*(3), 82.

Jones, C. a., & Shorter-Gooden, K. (2003). *Shifting: the double lives of Black women in America* (1st ed.). New York: HaperCollins.

Joshua, M. B. (2002). Inside picture books: where are the children of color? . *Educational Horizons, 80*(3).

Kasl, E., & Yorks, L. (2002). Collaborative inquiry for adult learning *New Directions for Adult and Continuing Education, 94*(Summer), 3-11.

Kirk, G., & Okazawa-Rey, M. (2001). *Women's lives: multicultural perspectives* (2nd ed.). MountainView, CA: Mayfield Publishing

Kirk, G., & Okazawa-Rey, M. (2003). *Women's lives: multicultural perspectives* (2nd ed.). MountainView, CA: Mayfield Publishing

Kleinfeld, J. (2002, 13 November 2006). Psychology Today: Six degrees: urban myth? March/April 2002. Retrieved October 23, 2007, from http://psychologytoday.com/articles/index.php?term=pto-20020301-000038&print=1

Kondo, D. (1997). *About face: performing race in fashion and theatre*. New York: Routledge.

Kwong, D. (2003). Beyond victimization. *Community Arts Network Reading Room* Retrieved April 23, 2007, from http://www.communityarts.net/readingroom/archivefiles/2003/10/beyond_victimiz.php

Lawson, M. H. (1988). *Women of color study Bible: created by and for contemporary women of African descent*. Iowa Falls, IA and Atlanta, GA: World Publishing, Iowa Falls, IA and Nia Publishing, Atlanta, GA.

Lindsey, K. (1970). The Black woman as a woman. In T. Cade (Ed.), *The Black Woman: An Anthology* (pp. 85-89). New York: Signet, NAL Penguin, Inc.

Lips, H. M. (1999). *"Women, Education, and Economic Participation." Keynote Address* Paper presented at the Northern Regional Seminar, National

Council of Women of New Zealand, Radford, Virginia.

Lipsky, S. (1987). *Internalized racism.* Rational Island: Seattle.

Livesay, J. (1989). Structuration theory and the unacknowledged conditions of action *Theory Culture & Society,* 6(2), 263-292.

Love, B. J. (1997). Learning to choose chitlins', *Internalized Oppression and the Development of a Liberatory Consciousness* (pp. 3). Amherst, MA: University of Massachusetts, Amherst.

Love, B. J. (2000). Developing a liberatory consciousness. In M. Adams, W. J. Blumenfield, R. Castaneda, H. W. Hackman, M. L. Peters & X. Zuniga (Eds.), *Reading for Diversity and Social Justice* (pp. 521). New York: Routledge.

Lynch, W. (1712). Let's make a slave. *Full Text of the Willie Lynch Writings* Retrieved September, 2001, from http://www.daveyd.com/willlynch.html

Mama, A. (1995). *Beyond the masks: race, gender and subjectivity* (First ed.). London: Routledge.

Marshall, C., & Rossman, G. B. (1999). *Designing qualitative research* (Third ed.). Thousand Oaks: SAGE Publications, Inc.

Maschner, H. D. G., & Reedy-Maschner, K. L. (2007). The taking and displaying of human body parts as trophies by Amerindians. *Interdisciplinary Contributions to Archaeology* Retrieved October 12, 2007, from http://www.springerlink.com/content/t12x162h26123451/

McCabe, D. E. L. (1988). Jezebel: the wicked queen. In M. H. Lawson (Ed.), *Women of Color Study Bible* (pp. 278-212). Iowa Falls, IA and Atlanta, GA: World Publishing, Iowa Falls, IA and Nia Publishing, Atlanta, GA.

Merriam-Webster. (2007). Merriam-Webster online collegiate dictionary, eleventh edition *Merriam-Webster Dictionary* Eleventh Edition Retrieved September, 2007, from http://www.m-w.com/dictionary

Neal-Barnett, A. (2003). Stress, anxiety, and strong Black women [Electronic Version]. *Buzzle Staff and Agencies,* Two. Retrieved March 23, 2007 from http://www.buzzle.com/editorials/9-6-2003-45076.asp.

Okazawa-Rey, M. (2003). Identities and social locations: Who am I? Who are my people? . In G. Kirk & M. Okazawa-Rey (Eds.), *Women's lives: multicultural perspectives* (2nd ed., pp. 49-59). MountainView, CA: Mayfield Publishing

Okazawa-Rey, M., et al. (1977). A Black feminist statement. *Combahee River Collective*, 7.

Okazawa-Rey, M., Robinson, T., & Ward, J. V. (1987). Black women and the politics of skin color and hair. *Women and Therapy*, 6, 89-102.

Omi, M., & Winant, H. (1994). *Racial formation in the United States: from 1960s to the 1990s* (2nd ed.). New York: Routledge.

Papper, B. (2005). Running in place: minorities and women in television see little change, while minorities fare worse in radio. *Communicator*, 26-32.

Parham, T. A. (1993). *Psychological storms: the African American struggle for identity*. Chicago, IL: African American Images.

Parham, T. A., White, J. L., & Ajamu, A., et al. (2000). *The psychology of Blacks: an African-centered perspective*. Upper Saddle River: Prentice Hall.

Parker, P. M. (2007). Webster's online dictionary. Retrieved March 31, 2007, 2007, from http://www.websters-online-dictionary.org/

Pastor, J., McCormick, J., Fine, M., Andolsen, R., Friedman, N., Richardson, N., et al. (1996). Makin' homes: an urban girl thing. In B. J. R. Leadbeater & N. Way (Eds.), *Urban girls: resisting stereotypes, creating identities* (pp. 15-33). New York: New York University.

Pierce, C. (1970). Offensive mechanisms. In F. B. Barbour (Ed.), *The Black seventies* (pp. 335). Boston, MA: Porter Sargent.

Pyant, C. J. Y., Barbara J. . (1991). Relationship of racial identity and gender-role attitudes to Black women's psychological well-being. *Journal of Counseling Psychology, 38*(3), 7.

Randall, V. (2004). Gender and the law - course summary. *Gender & Law: Theory, Doctrine, Commentary* Retrieved April 22, 2007, from http://

academic.udayton.edu/gender/01Unit/index.htm

Reid, P. T. (2004). A postscript for research on Black women; new populations, new directions. *Journal of Black Psychology, 30*(3), 443-446.

Rhymes, E. (2005). Black Identity and Black Unity Retrieved April 23, 2007, from http://www.blackcommentator.com/134/134_black_identidy_1.html

Rosenberg, R. (2002). The conjunction of race and gender. *Journal of Women's History, 14*(2), 7.

Rowland, D. (2004). *The boundaries of her body: the troubling history of women's rights in America* (1st ed.). Naperville, IL: Sphinx Publishing, an imprint of Sourcebooks, Inc.

Scott, K. Y. (1991). *The habit of surviving: Black women's strategies for life.* New Brunswick: Rutgers University Press.

Sennett, R., & Cobb, J. (1973). *The hidden injuries of class.* New York: Vintage Books.

Sheldrake, R. (1995). *The presence of the past: Morphic resonance and the habits of nature* (Second ed.). Rochester, VT: Park Street Press.

Shorter-Gooden, K. (2004). Multiple resistance strategies: how African American women cope with racism and sexism. *Journal of Black Psychology* 30(3), 19.

Shorter-Gooden, K., & Washington, N. C. (1996). Young, Black and female: the challenge of weaving an identity. *Journal of Adolescence, 19*(5), 465-475.

Smith, L. (2002). Using the power of collaborative inquiry: community women learn and lead themselves. *New Directions for Adult and Continuing Education, 94*(Summer), 23-32.

Smitherman, G. (1999). *Talkin that talk: language, culture, and education in African America* (First ed.). New York, NY: Routledge.

Solorzano, D., Ceja, M., & Yossa, T. (2000). Critical race theory, racial microaggressions, and campus racial climate: the experiences of African American college students. *Journal of Negro Education.*

Spencer, M. B. (1988). Self concept and development. In D. T. Slaughter (Ed.), *Perspectives on black child development: new directions for child development* (pp. 59-72). San Francisco: Jossey-Bass.

Spencer, M. B. (1990). Development of minority children: an introduction. *Child Development, 61*, 267-269.

Spencer, M. B., & Markstrom-Adams, C. (1990). Identity processes among racial and ethnic minority children in America. *Child Development, 61*, 290-310.

Spring, J. H. (2004). *Deculturalization and the struggle for equality: a brief history of the education of dominated cultures in the United States* (Fourth ed.). New York: McGraw-Hill.

St. Jean, Y., & Feagin, J. R. (1998). *Double burden: Black women and everyday racism* (First ed.). Armonk, New York: M. E. Sharpe, Inc.

Stacey, R. D. (2001). *Complex responsive processes in organizations: learning and knowledge creation* (First ed.). New York: Routledge.

Stephens, D. P., & Phillips, L. (2005). Integrating Black feminist thought into conceptual frameworks of African American adolescent women's sexual scripting processes. *Sexualities, Evolution and Gender,* 7(1), 37-55.

Thomas, V. (2004). The psychology of Black women: studying Black women's lives in context. *Journal of Black Psychology,* 30(3), 20.

Travis, M. A. (2003). Detach to power: the collective memory-work experience (pp. 236): The Fielding Graduate Institute.

Truth, S. (1851). Ain't I a woman. *Women's Convention* Retrieved June 2, 2006, from http://www.feminist.com/resources/artspeech/genwom/sojour.htm

Ward, J. V. (1996). Raising resisters: the role of truth telling in the psychological development of African American girls. In B. J. R. Leadbeater & N. Way (Eds.), *Urban girls: resisting stereotypes, creating identities* (pp. 85-99). New York: New York University Press.

Way, N. (1998). *Everyday courage: the lives and stories of urban teenagers* (first ed.). New York: New York University Press.

White, D. G. (1999). *Ar'n't I a woman?* (First ed.). New York: W. W. Norton & Company, Inc.

Williams, L. (2000). *It's the little things: everyday interactions that anger, annoy and divide the races.* New York: Harcourt.

Wilson, A. N. (1978). *The developmental psychology of the Black child.* New York: African Research Publications.

Woodson, C. G. (1933). *The Mis-education of the Negro* (First ed.). Chicago: African American Images.

Yi, K., & Shorter-Gooden, K. (1999). Ethnic identity formation: from stage theory to a constructivist narrative model. *Psychotherapy, 36*(1), 16-26.

Yoshino, K. (2006). *Covering: the hidden assault on our civil rights* (1st ed.). New York: Random House.

Dr. Ruth D. Edwards

About the Author

Dr. Ruth Edwards is a Critical Social Theorist and a Human Development Scholar. She studies the effect culture has on socio-psychological development and examines human behavior to discover 'why people do what they do'. Her research on US-born Black Women's socialization resulted in the creation of a theory in the human development canon known as Internalized Collective Consciousness, which is specific to Black Women.

She is the Director of Education at the Winter Park Library, working with a team of 14 librarians to produce learning experiences for age infants to infinity. She has worked as an organizational consultant in social justice and inclusion, a project manager producing interactive videodisc training, and spent twelve years in broadcasting as a radio announcer and producer-host of a live, weekly women's television program and a quarterly community affairs television program.

Dr. Edwards is an alumnus of the Oxford International Roundtable and is published on two continents. She earned a PhD in Human

Development and Master of Arts in Organizational Systems, from Fielding Graduate University; a Master of Science in Education, from Southern Illinois University at Carbondale with a concentration in Telecommunications; and a Bachelor of Arts in Communication Arts, from Johnson C. Smith University.

Ruth is a native of Awendaw, S.C., currently residing in Central Florida. She enjoys reading everything, listening to music and audiobooks, and taking in blue water and white sand wherever she finds it.

Milton Keynes UK
Ingram Content Group UK Ltd.
UKHW021942281024
450365UK00018B/1237